REVISE

PSYCHOLOGY FOR GCSE LEVEL

DIANA JACKSON-DWYER & CRAIG ROBERTS

Psychology Press
Taylor & Francis Group
HOVE AND NEW YORK

Published 2010
by Psychology Press
27 Church Road, Hove, East Sussex BN3 2FA

Simultaneously published in the USA and Canada
by Psychology Press
270 Madison Avenue, New York, NY 10016

Psychology Press is an imprint of the Taylor & Francis group, an Informa business

British Library Cataloguing in Publication Data
A catalogue record for this book is available from the British Library

ISBN: 978-1-84872-048-0

Typeset in the UK by RefineCatch Ltd, Bungay, Suffolk
Cover design by Andy Ward
Printed and bound in the UK by Ashford Colour Press Ltd., Gosport, Hampshire

R E V I S E

PSYCHOLOGY FOR GCSE LEVEL

DIANA JACKSON-DWYER

To Bena and Carly, who have responded enthusiastically to conditioning and have trained their owners so well.

CRAIG ROBERTS

This book is for everyone who loves studying the wonders of psychology, plus Jav, Jayney, Julieníque, Martinez, Elle, Graham and of course Wiggy. Naturally, everything I do is for my lovely family.

CONTENTS

PREPARING FOR THE GCSE EXAM

About your GCSE course

The OCR GCSE is made up of three units, which we will refer to as Units 1, 2 and 3, with one exam per unit.

The units		
Unit 1: Studies and Applications in Psycholoy 1	**Unit 2: Studies and Applications in Psychology 2**	**Unit 3: Research in Psychology**
Biological psychology: sex and gender	Biological psychology: criminal behaviour	Planning research
Cognitive psychology: memory	Cognitive psychology: perception	Doing research
Developmental psychology: attachment	Developmental psychology: cognitive development	Analysing research
Social psychology: obedience	Social psychology: non-verbal communication	Planning an investigation
Individual differences: atypical behaviour	Individual differences: the self	

The exam papers		
Paper 1 (examines Unit 1)	**Paper 2 (examines Unit 2)**	**Paper 3 (examines Unit 3)**
80 marks	**80 marks**	**40 marks**
1 hour 15 min	**1 hour 15 min**	**1 hour**
Five sections: one per approach	**Five sections: one per approach**	**Two sections**
The topic areas can be in any order. Four of the five sections are worth 15 marks each, and the fifth section is worth 20 marks	The topic areas can be in any order. Four of the five sections are worth 15 marks each, and the fifth section is worth 20 marks	**Section A** is worth 25 marks. You are given some source material (e.g. an account of a study) and asked a series of questions around it

(continued overleaf)

Paper 1 (examines Unit 1)	Paper 2 (examines Unit 2)	Paper 3 (examines Unit 3)
The first three sections contain only short-answer questions, with questions worth between 1 and 4 marks each. The fourth section also consists of short-answer questions but the last question is worth 6 marks. The last section is worth 20 marks, with the last question being 10 marks	The first three sections contain only short-answer questions, with questions worth between 1 and 4 marks each. The fourth section also consists of short-answer questions but the last question is worth 6 marks. The last section is worth 20 marks, with the last question being 10 marks	**Section B** is worth 15 marks and requires you to plan a study. You will be told what method to use (e.g. an observation, questionnaire, interview, experiment)

Summary of OCR GCSE Psychology exam papers			
	Paper 1	**Paper 2**	**Paper 3**
How long?	1 hour 15 min	1 hour 15 min	1 hour
Per cent of whole GCSE	40%	40%	20%
Total number of marks	80	80	40
Number of sections	Five	Five	Two

Quality of written communication (QWC)

You will be examined on the quality of your writing. This means that, in order to maximise your marks in an exam, you should:

- Make sure that your writing is legible (that it can be read) and that spelling, punctuation and grammar are accurate so that the meaning is clear.
- Organise the information clearly. Try to avoid bullet points where possible and write in full sentences with appropriate use of capital letters and full stops. On the longer answers, paragraph your work.
- Use psychological terms wherever possible and appropriate.
- Do NOT use text language!

On the exam paper, for some of the longer questions you will be asked to write "in continuous prose". This is an indication that QWC will be assessed in the answer. Be particularly careful to avoid using note form or bullet points in these answers because this will reduce your QWC marks. (In the other answers you probably will not lose marks by using bullet points, but it's a good habit to try to avoid them so that you are not tempted to use them on the answers in which QWC is assessed.)

	Examples of how NOT to write to gain marks for QWC	Examples of how to write to gain marks for QWC
Writing should be legible	*[handwritten]* A definition of aggression in the intention to harm other people.	*[handwritten]* A definition of aggression is the intention to harm other people.
Spelling, punctuation and grammar should be correct	Femals have 2X cromasomes and men has XY this is what makes them men and women	Females have XX chromosomes whilst males have XY. These are sex chromosomes, which are responsible for the sex of the individual
Use psychological terms	There's not much room in your immediate memory	Short-term memory has a small capacity, about seven items
	People don't like it if u stand 2 close	People become uncomfortable if their personal space is invaded
	Milgram should not have lied to people	Milgram has been criticised for deceiving the participants

Revision

Organise yourself

1. Know exactly what you have to learn for each of your exams.
2. Make sure you have notes on everything. There is no choice of questions in the exam, so be aware that you need to know everything.
3. Make a list of what you need to learn. You can tick things off as you go.
4. Look at past papers.
5. Sort out the times you will revise. Try to allow a reasonable length of time but give yourself frequent short breaks. Do about 30 minutes and then take a 5-minute break. Repeat this for three sessions and then take a good break (at least half an hour).
6. Sort out a quiet, comfortable place to revise. If home is too noisy, try the local library.

How to revise

There are many ways to revise – the key is to find a method that suits you.

Suggested revision activities

Write revision notes
Revision notes are brief notes made from your class notes or a textbook. The key is that you reword them (don't just copy), as this means you have to understand what you are writing and this is crucial for remembering. When you write your notes, make them well organised (lots of numbered points) and visually memorable – use different colours and illustrations that might help you to remember.

Summarise the main studies
In an exam you may have to summarise a study in a few lines. Always learn core studies in terms of aim, method, findings, conclusion.

Draw pictures

Whenever possible, draw pictures to illustrate what you are trying to remember. For example, draw labelled storage jars for the multistore model of memory, each jar representing one store and surrounded by pictures that illustrate the characteristics of the store.

Do mind maps

This is a different way of writing revision notes. Mind maps are useful for seeing an overview of a topic; they really do help to summarise the whole topic area and to see how concepts fit together.

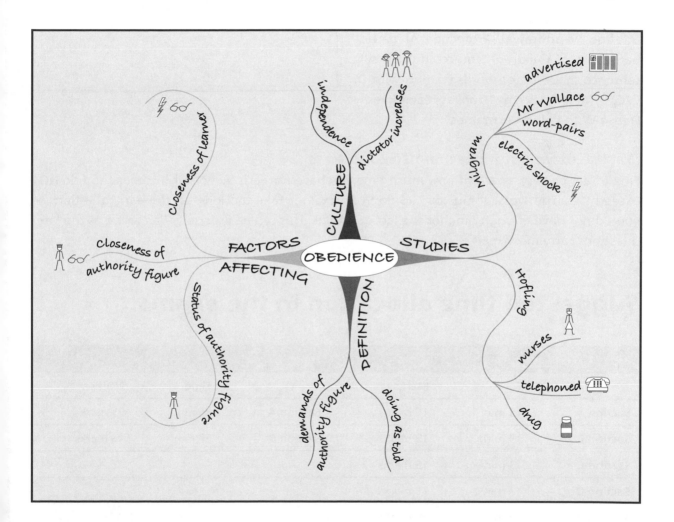

Make revision cards

Write a question or concept on one side and the answer on the other. With respect to methods, you could do three cards for each method (observation, questionnaire and so on), one asking for the definition, one for an advantage and one for a disadvantage.

Do more than just read

Repeat what you've read. Close your eyes and recite what you have just said. Then do it again.

Use memory tricks

Use rhymes, silly associations, etc. The more ridiculous, unusual and distinctive they are, the better the information will stick in your memory. For example, for ethical guidelines (Deception, Consent, Confidentiality, Debriefing, Withdrawal, Protection of participants, use of Children), you could use a silly sentence made up of words starting with D, C, C, D, W, P, C, such as "Donkeys Can Clumsily Dance With Police Constables".

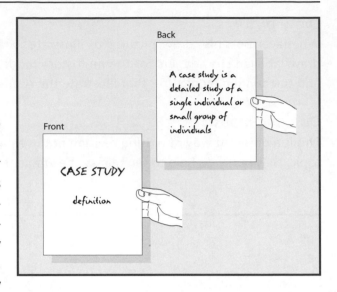

Practise exam questions in timed conditions

First of all, be very aware of how much time you have for each section of the exam and do NOT exceed this. The worst thing you can do in an exam is take too long on the early questions so you do not have enough time for the last questions. This can be especially damaging as the later questions carry more marks.

Suggested time allocation in the exams

Paper 1 and Paper 2			Paper 3		
	Time	Marks		Time	Marks
Section A	13 min	15 marks	Section A	35 min	25 marks
Section B	13 min	15 marks	Section B	20 min	15 marks
Section C	13 min	15 marks			
Section D	13 min	15 marks			
Section E	18 min	20 marks			
Checking	5 min		Checking	5 min	
Total	1 hour 15 min	80 marks	Total	1 hour	40 marks

In the exam

Read the questions very carefully

Make sure you know what you are being asked to do. Some important points to note are as follows:

- Describing studies: You are used to studies being in terms of aim, method, results, conclusion. You may be asked for only one section (e.g. Outline the findings of . . .). Make sure that's all you write about. If asked to describe a study with the instruction to use continuous prose, make sure you do NOT use side-headings. Still approach the answer in terms of the sections, but write in sentences and paragraphs.
- If asked to evaluate, do not describe.
- If asked to describe and evaluate (either a theory or a study), be especially careful not to spend all the time you have on describing and do no evaluation, or vice versa.
- If the question gives you an article (a short paragraph on a topic area) or a piece of conversation and asks questions on it, make sure you refer to the article or conversation throughout.
- When answering true/false questions, read the statements very carefully. Many students have thrown away marks by careless reading.
- Questions that start "From your study of psychology" require you to write about *studies* or *theories* you have learnt. For example:
  Question: From your study of psychology outline two reasons why people obey authority. (4)
  Answer: Do NOT make up "common sense" reasons from your everyday experience. Use your psychology! A suitable answer would be as follows: "From his research, Milgram identified a number of reasons why people obeyed. One reason was the power of the situation. There is a very strong social expectation that participants will do what the experimenter (authority figure) asks them to do in an experiment, especially as the participants have volunteered and been paid to take part in the study. Another reason why participants obeyed in this situation was that they did not feel responsible for what they were doing. They feel that it is the person in authority who is responsible for the action."
- Some questions require you to fill in missing words, or draw lines between boxes, etc. Read the instructions carefully and make sure you do what is asked. If you do happen to make a mistake, cross out what you have done very clearly, so the examiner is certain of your final answer.

Look at the mark allocation for each question

This gives you a really strong clue as to how much you should write. If a question is only worth 1 mark you should be very brief. If it is worth 4 marks you obviously need to write more. Think about your answer from the examiner's point of view – have you given enough detail for them to award you all the available marks? If you have not, try to expand your answer, perhaps by giving an example to illustrate what you mean.

What not to do in the exam

GOOD LUCK!

BIOLOGICAL PSYCHOLOGY: Sex and Gender

2

What's it about?

Biological psychology is an approach that emphasises the role of biological factors, such as genetics, hormones, evolution and brain function, in the study of our behaviour. Therefore, our behaviours could be controlled by biological mechanisms. The area of focus for this chapter is sex and gender, and what factors may control our "sense" of being a male or female. What causes typical development, and reasons why people may wish to change their sex, are also considered in this topic.

WHAT'S IN THIS UNIT?

The specification lists the following things that you will need to be able to do for the examination:

- Distinguish between sex and gender
- Outline concepts of masculinity, femininity and androgyny
- Outline the role of chromosomes in typical gender development
- Outline the role of gonads and hormone production in typical gender development
- Describe basic evolutionary sex differences in human behaviour
- Explain the criticisms of the biological theory of gender development
- Consider psychoanalytical theory as an alternative theory with specific reference to the role of the Oedipus/Electra complex in gender development
- Describe and outline limitations of the Diamond and Sigmundson (1997) study
- Outline an application of research into sex and gender, e.g. single-sex schooling

Key terms

Here is a list of important terms that you should learn in your revision. Try to write definitions for these after reading the chapter, and check your answers in the glossary on pp. 129–135. Essential terms that you *must* know in order to properly understand the topic are marked with an asterisk.

Androgyny*	Hormones	Penis envy
Castration anxiety	Introjection	Sex identity*
Chromosomes	Libido	Sex typing
Electra complex	Masculinity*	Testosterone
Femininity*	Oedipus complex	
Gender identity*	Oestrogen	

Some important definitions

The distinction between sex and gender

- **Sex identity**: This term refers to the *biological* status of being a male or a female. This is based on chromosomes and genitals.

- ■ Remember – when psychologists refer to *sex* they mean the *biological* status of a person.

- **Gender identity**: This term refers to the *psychological* status of being a male or a female. It includes an awareness of which gender you consider yourself.

- ■ Remember – when psychologists refer to *gender* they mean the *psychological* status of a person.

The concepts of masculinity, femininity and androgyny

These terms refer to treating people in accordance with society's expectations of them because of their sex.

- **Masculinity**: This term refers to the behaviours and ideas that are considered to be a characteristic of being male. It is an example of sex typing.
- **Femininity**: This term refers to the behaviours and ideas that are considered to be a characteristic of being female. It is also an example of sex typing.

- **Androgyny**: This term was introduced by a psychologist called Sandra Bem (1974). It refers to a set of behaviours that include high levels of both masculine and feminine characteristics.

■ Remember – when psychologists refer to *androgyny* they mean the *psychological* status of a person, not their *biological* status.

The role of chromosomes in typical gender development

Males	Females
XY chromosomes	XX chromosomes
Y from sperm	X from sperm
This dictates growth of sexual organs and testosterone	This dictates growth of sexual organs and oestrogen

Also, it should be noted that it is the release of sex hormones at about 8 weeks into pregnancy that determines our biological sex. All embryos prior to this time are actually female and it is only the release of testosterone that makes the female sex organs develop into male sex organs.

The role of gonads and hormone production in typical gender development

We will look at the role of *two* hormones: **oestrogen** (females) and **testosterone** (males).

Males	Females
Testosterone	Oestrogen
Required for sperm production, the development of male reproductive organs Involved in the production of facial hair, the deepening of the voice and muscle growth	Required for sexual development, puberty, the stimulation of egg production and female reproductive organs
Produced in the testes and adrenal glands	Produced in the ovaries

Basic evolutionary sex differences in human behaviour

Evolution would state that any differences between males and females have developed to help the human species survive.

- If the behaviour is seen in many cultures then we could believe that this behaviour has evolved in humans in general.
- If a behaviour is very different across cultures then we could conclude that it is the result of a person's upbringing and not evolution.

Evidence

Study	Findings for males	Findings for females
Geary (1999)	Males will choose more mates in total than women and show a preference for youth and beauty (e.g. short-term benefits)	Females typically choose mates who are physically, genetically and behaviourally fit. Therefore, they choose a mate who will be strong enough to benefit them in the long term
Lippa (2005)	Show higher levels of aggression, especially physical	Show much lower levels of physical aggression
	Males better at visuo-spatial tasks. The reason for this could be the evolution of a part of our brain called the *hippocampus*. It has evolved differently in males and females, bringing about the differences highlighted	Not as good at visuo-spatial skills
Barry, Bacon and Child (1957)	Stronger achievement drive	More responsible
	More self-reliant	More nurturing

Criticisms of the biological theory of gender development

- It is reductionist. It reduces all of our behaviour down to chromosomes, genetics and hormones. Therefore, it ignores other factors that may well affect our gender development.
- Also, certain individuals may not have their sex identity and gender identity the same (e.g. they have the genitalia of a man but feel like a woman). If the biological theory was fully correct then this could not happen as it should control both sex and gender. Clearly this does not always happen.

Psychoanalytical theory as an alternative

- Freud believed that early experiences plus our unconscious mind helped us to develop our sense of being a male or a female.
- Libido (sex drive) is with us from birth.
- The "energy" created has to be "used up" in socially appropriate ways.
- So, for the first year our libido is centred on our mouth (called the oral phase).
- This moves onto the anus (called the anal phase) as we get a bit older.
- By the age of 3–4 years it shifts to the penis in boys and clitoris in girls (the phallic stage). During this latter stage Freud believed that we develop our sense of gender.

Males	Females
Oedipus complex	Oedipus complex (sometimes referred to as Electra Complex)
Boy's libido creates some sort of "desire" for the opposite-sex parent	Girl has the same unconscious desires for her father
Father may become angry if he finds out about this desire	But, she also fears the loss of her mother's love
The boy does not necessarily know this as it may happen in his unconscious	The girl does not necessarily know this as it may happen in her unconscious
Boy fears that his father will castrate him, causing castration anxiety	Noticing that her mother does not have a penis, the girl experiences penis envy
Gets rid of his anxieties by identifying with his father	She feels that she has already been castrated
Boy introjects the father's personality and adopts many gender roles attached to being a male	She then introjects her mother's personality and adopts many gender roles attached to being a female

EVALUATION

➕ Freud studied a boy called Little Hans who had a fear of horses as they reminded him of his father. Once he had identified with his father by resolving the Oedipus conflict, the phobia disappeared and he began to act in a sex-typed way.

➖ As we are dealing with unconscious mechanisms, it is virtually impossible to test out the theory directly.

➖ There are alternative more plausible theories that can explain gender-appropriate behaviour, such as social learning theory and gender schema theory.

CORE STUDY: DIAMOND AND SIGMUNDSON (1997)

Aim: This case study is a long-term follow-up of a child who underwent sex reassignment at birth.

Background to the case: The penis of an 8-month-old boy was accidentally damaged during an operation and he was then subsequently raised as a female. According to medical texts, the common theory is that it is easier to make a good vagina than a good penis. Therefore, if in doubt, conduct surgery to construct a vagina and raise the child as a girl.

Follow-up findings: See p.143 of *Psychology for GCSE Level, 2nd Edition*, for fuller findings.

(1) Individuals are psychosexually neutral at birth: One of the strongest memories reported by John's mother was post-surgery. She was told to treat him like a girl. But this was a disaster – as soon as she put a dress on Joan she ripped it off. At times Joan could act feminine, being neat and tidy. However, in one incident, herself and her twin brother would rather mimic their father shaving than their mother applying make-up. Her mother tried to "correct" the behaviour but this was unsuccessful. At the age of 14 Joan told one of her doctors that she had suspected she was a boy for a long time. Shortly after this, Joan decided to switch to living as a male. She had a mastectomy at the age of 14 and phallus construction at the ages of 15 and 16.

(2) Healthy psychosexual development is intimately related to the appearance of genitals: When Joan expressed feelings about not wanting to be a girl she was ridiculed by her therapists. She continually felt embarrassed as she was forced to expose her vagina repeatedly in check-ups to make sure everything was alright and to see whether more repairs were needed. She had meetings with male-to-female transsexuals to convince her of the advantages of being a girl. After one such meeting when she was aged 13, Joan ran away from the hospital and was found hiding on a nearby roof. With continued therapy to help her generate a female identity, Joan kept thinking that she was being treated as a "freak". At the age of 14,

Joan could take no more and refused to live as a girl. She began to wear gender-neutral clothes like jeans and shirts, and Inkblot tests showed that Joan was thinking more like a boy than a girl. John still cannot believe the narrow-mindedness of people for thinking that his entire personality was linked to the presence or absence of a penis!

Conclusion: It would appear that individuals are *not* psychosexually neutral at birth (so we cannot simply make them switch sex). Also, there is more to healthy psychosexual development than what genitals a person has.

Limitations:

- As this is a case study of one boy it could be difficult to generalise to other children who have had similar experiences. There may be something unique about John and his experiences.
- Also, long-term follow-ups like this one have to rely on the participants' memories. These may not be as accurate as if they had been followed during the process.
- Finally, with interviews there may be interviewer bias where questions are worded in a particular way to generate answers that researchers want to hear rather than what the participant truly wants to say.

Application: Single-sex schooling

Sadker and Sadker (1995) noted that girls tend to receive less attention and less encouragement from teachers compared with boys. However, boys tend to be more assertive and disruptive and they will try to dominate the use of resources such as computers and science equipment, so the teacher has no choice but to pay more attention to them!

Lippa (2005) noted the following recommendations:

- *Boys*: Use after-school tutoring, create workshops to help boys with social skills and find ways for boys to channel aggression more effectively (e.g. sports leagues at lunchtime or after school)
- *Girls*: Create workshops to encourage maths and science, use field trips to expose girls to female role models and teach women's studies.

Is single-sex schooling the answer?

- There is some evidence to suggest that all-girls schools do encourage more interest in maths and science.
- However, some psychologists argue that the girls who *choose* to attend same-sex schools bring about these effects themselves rather than the school itself.
- Girls who choose same-sex schools tend to be better motivated, have higher academic abilities and have less interest in less academic social activities.

- Research shows that same-sex schools for boys provide higher levels of structure and discipline, which reduces behavioural problems.
- However, being in a same-sex environment may just enhance things like toughness, hierarchies in terms of dominance and ingroup–outgroup conflict.
- With boys being separated from girls, some research has shown that the boys are *more* likely to see girls as sex objects.

OVER TO YOU

Now try the following revision activities:

1. On post-it notes, write down the behaviours that are different between males and females under the evolutionary section on p.12 (e.g. more aggressive, more responsible). Then mix them up and try to put them under a male and female column on a large piece of paper. Do the same with the features of psychodynamic theory so you can then understand the differences between males and females.
2. Using index cards, write down all of the essential terms on one side and their definitions on the reverse. Get someone to test you on them.

EXAMPLE EXAM QUESTIONS

1 Distinguish between sex and gender using an example. **3 MARKS**

2 Describe **two** basic evolutionary sex differences in human behaviour. **4 MARKS**

3 What was the aim of the Diamond and Sigmundson (1997) case study? **2 MARKS**

4 Describe and evaluate the biological theory of gender development. **8 MARKS**

MODEL ANSWER TO QUESTION 3

The aim of the Diamond and Sigmundson (1997) study was to conduct a long-term follow-up on a child who had undergone a sex change after birth to see what effects it had on them.

COGNITIVE PSYCHOLOGY:
Memory

What's it about?

Cognitive psychology is all about how internal (mental) processes affect our behaviours and experiences. It focuses on things like memory, perception, language and attention. Behaviours that we may feel are simple do involve complex mental processes. Just finding your way from A to B requires the skills of memory, paying attention and using your perceptual system to understand the world around you!

WHAT'S IN THIS UNIT?

The specification lists the following things that you will need to be able to do for the examination:

- Describe information processing as encoding (input), storage and retrieval (output)
- Distinguish between accessibility and availability problems in memory
- Distinguish between sensory store (buffer), short-term memory and long-term memory with reference to duration and capacity
- Describe the processes of attention and rehearsal
- Explain how forgetting occurs through decay and displacement
- Consider levels of processing as an alternative theory
- Describe and know the limitations of Terry's (2005) study
- Application of research into memory, e.g. memory aids

Key terms

Here is a list of important terms that you should learn in your revision. Try to write definitions for these after reading the chapter, and check your answers in the glossary on pp. 129–135. Essential terms that you *must* know in order to properly understand the topic are marked with an asterisk.

Accessibility	Imagery	Rehearsal
Availability	Levels of processing	Retrieval (output)*
Brain damage	Long-term memory	Semantic processing
Cue dependency	Method of loci	Sensory buffer
Decay	Mind maps	Short-term memory
Displacement	Organisation	Storage*
Encoding (input)*	Phonemic/phonetic	Structural processing
Hierarchies	processing	

Some important definitions

- **Encoding (input)** means that we create a memory trace when presented with material (this could be visual, sound, smell, etc.). So, it is the taking in of information through our senses.
- **Storage** refers to where we keep the information that we have encoded and then processed in some way (e.g. rehearsed the information). So, it is keeping information that we can then use again if necessary.
- **Retrieval (output)** involves us finding information that we have *encoded* and then *stored* in the brain. It means getting information from our memory system that we can then use.

Accessibility and availability problems in memory

Accessibility problems linked to memory are all about attempting to find information that has already been processed. A person may think they have forgotten the information completely but the real reason is that they simply cannot access it.

Availability problems linked to memory are all about losing information that may have already been processed in the brain. Therefore it is no longer *available*, as it has disappeared for good.

Multistore model of memory

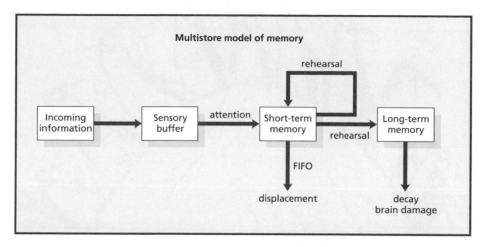

- The **sensory buffer** picks up information based around our senses.
- This information is only taken further if we pay *attention* to it.
- If we pay attention to the information then it can enter our **short-term memory (STM)**. This has a limited capacity – it is believed that it can hold seven plus or minus two items. Memories last from 15 to 30 seconds
- Once the amount of information goes above the maximum amount that can fit into our STM, **displacement** happens – the item that was first into your STM will be the first out (FIFO, First In First Out)!
- If we **rehearse/repeat** the information then it could go into **long-term memory**. Here it can be stored indefinitely and potentially lasts forever.
- **Decay** can happen, where the information simply gets more and more faint, or **brain damage**, where the memories that were physically stored in the brain are literally taken out.

EVALUATION

➕ There is some supporting evidence for the limited capacity of short-term memory (Glanzer & Cunitz, 1966; see pp. 219–220 of *Psychology for GCSE Level, 2nd Edition*).

➕ Case studies of brain-damaged patients can lend support to there being separate short-term and long-term memory stores (see pp. 225–226 of *Psychology for GCSE Level, 2nd Edition*, for examples).

➖ Atkinson and Shiffrin may have been incorrect about the potential capacity of short-term memory (Boutla et al., 2004; see p. 219 of *Psychology for GCSE Level, 2nd Edition*).

➖ The multistore model cannot explain how some distinctive information gets into long-term memory without going through the processes highlighted in it.

First in, first out!

Levels of processing

Craik and Lockhart (1974) stated that memories are a by-product of the way in which we process information. They proposed three different levels of processing:

1. **Structural**. This refers to processing things in relation to the way they look (e.g. the structure of things).
2. **Phonemic/phonetic**. This refers to processing things in relation to how they sound.
3. **Semantic**. This refers to processing things in relation to what they mean.

An example to help you

- *Structural*: Is the following word in lower case? GUITAR
- *Phonemic*: Does the following word rhyme with horse? force
- Semantic: Does the following word fit into the sentence "Is _____ a type of vegetable"? carrot

CORE STUDY: TERRY (2005)

Aim: Terry asked the question *". . . does the position of a television commercial in a block of commercials determine how well it will be recalled?"* (p.151).

Method:

- *Experiment 1*: There were four lists of 15 advertisements, which gave a total of 60 advertisements used in the study. There were local and national brands. Half of the advertisements lasted 15 seconds and the other half 30 seconds. All advertisements were for different products and companies. Participants were tested on recall three times – immediately after being presented with the advertisements, after completing a 3-minute verbal assessment test and then after they had completed their research participation form.
- *Experiment 2*: There were three lists of advertisements labelled A, B and C. The participants were asked to watch a comedy show and the programme was stopped at 4, 8 and 15 minutes when the advertisements were presented. The programme was then stopped at 18 minutes and the participants were asked to recall as many of the advertisements as possible.
- *Experiment 3*: Experiment 2 was repeated with a separate sample of 23 students, but instead of a recall task at 18 minutes they were given a recognition task.

Results:

- *Experiment 1*: When the participants were tested immediately they recalled more from the beginning and the end of the list (called the *primacy–recency* effect). As soon as the participants had to complete any task (the verbal task and the form filling) the advertisements at the end of the list were not remembered very well. There was no difference in whether the advertisements were 15 seconds or 30 seconds long.
- *Experiments 2 and 3*: Participants were good at recalling advertisements that happened at the beginning of the list. For the recognition task there was little effect of position in the advertisement list.

Conclusion: Advertisements that appeared in the first three or four positions in a list of 15 were recalled better. Therefore, advertisers should want their products to be advertised then, and television companies could charge more for these "prime" positions in a commercial break!

Limitations:

- Small sample with a slight gender imbalance in each experiment. This could affect the results, as Terry did not test whether females were more likely to have better recall for products aimed at females, and vice versa for males.
- The initial experiment (i.e. just watching advertisements and nothing else!) was nothing like how we view advertisements when we watch our favourite television shows. However, he did attempt to change this in Experiments 2 and 3 by making the advertisements appear during a television show.

Memory aids

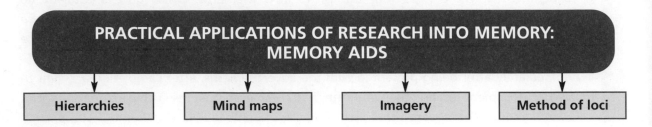

Hierarchies

With this technique, material that you wish to learn is placed into a hierarchy. The hierarchy begins with something general and the further down the hierarchy you go, the more specific the information is. You may wish to try this with a topic of your choice.

Evidence

Bower, Clark, Lesgold and Winzenz (1969) asked people to learn words that had been placed into a hierarchy diagram or not. For those in the organised group, their average recall was 73 words. For the random group, their recall averaged only 21.

Mind maps

According to Buzan (2005), "a Mind Map is the easiest way to put information into your brain and take information out of the brain" (p. 6). He compares mind maps to the map of a city. The centre of a mind map is like the centre of a city, as it represents the main idea. The main roads out of the city represent the main areas of information we are wishing to learn. The further out of the city we go, the more roads appear and this represents more information and thoughts. An example of a mind map can be seen on p. 5 of this revision guide.

Imagery and memory

One way that we can use *imagery* to help us to recall information is to visualise images of the material.

Evidence

Bower and Winzenz (1970) gave participants word pairs to learn. Group 1 participants were simply told to repeat the pairs several times. Group 2 participants were asked to construct a mental picture of the two words interacting. The latter group recalled over twice as many word pairs as the first group.

Wollen, Weber and Lowry (1972) wanted to see if bizarreness in imagery helps us to recall word pairs. Participants were split into four groups:

1. Images interacting and bizarre.
2. Images interacting but not bizarre.
3. Images not interacting but bizarre.
4. Images not interacting and not bizarre.

Interestingly, if the images were interacting, recall improved. Bizarreness did not improve recall any further.

Method of loci

Bower (1970) highlighted the steps that should be used in this technique:

1. Memorise a list of locations that are already arranged in a logical order. A good example could be your route to school, college or workplace.
2. Create an image for each item of information that you wish to remember.
3. Take these items in the order that you feel they need to be learned and associate them in turn with locations you have chosen.

Evidence

Groninger (1971) tested out the method of loci with a list of 25 words. Group 1 participants were asked to use a familiar route and place the 25 words along it. The second group were simply asked to try to remember the 25 words in any way they liked. At both 1 and 5 weeks after the learning phase, Group 1 (the method of loci group) recalled more words.

OVER TO YOU

Now try the following revision activities:

1. Using *any one* of the memory aids, take an area (e.g. theories of memory) and create a mind map, use imagery, etc.
2. For the multistore model of memory, buy some index cards. Write the words *capacity, storage, forgetting*, etc. on one side of the card and then the answers on the other side. Get someone to read out one side of the card and then you guess what is on the other side.

EXAMPLE EXAM QUESTIONS

1 Define the term *encoding* using an example. **3 MARKS**

2 What is the difference between accessibility problems and availability problems in memory? **3 MARKS**

3 Outline **two** memory aids that you know about. **6 MARKS**

4 Describe **two** results from the Terry (2005) study. **4 MARKS**

MODEL ANSWER TO QUESTION 4

The first result is from Experiment 1. The participants, when simply asked to recall the adverts they had seen, could remember those at the beginning and the end of the list better than the adverts in the middle (called the primacy–recency effect). The second result also comes from Experiment 1. When the participants had to complete a task after seeing the adverts (e.g. form filling), those adverts at the end of the list were poorly recalled.

DEVELOPMENTAL PSYCHOLOGY: Attachment

4

What's it about?

Human infants appear to have an instinctive need to form an attachment bond with a caring adult. In this chapter we consider the nature of this attachment bond and what biological purpose it serves. We then go deeper and look at what might happen if this bond is disrupted or never formed. Is it likely that children who are neglected in early life may be prone to an uncaring personality or even a life of crime? Can short-term separation be harmful to children's emotional development? These are just two of the important questions posed by the research discussed in this section. Finally, we consider some of the practical applications to which this research can be put.

WHAT'S IN THIS UNIT?

The specification lists the following things that you will need to be able to do for the examination:

- Describe separation protest and stranger anxiety as measures of attachment
- Distinguish between different types of attachment: secure, insecure-avoidant, insecure-ambivalent
- Explain the concept of monotropy
- Explain the concept of a critical period in attachment
- Describe the effects of attachment, deprivation and privation
- Explain the criticisms of Bowlby's theory of attachment
- Consider behaviourist theory as an alternative theory, with specific reference to reinforcement in attachment as opposed to instinct
- Describe Hazan and Shaver's survey of the relationship between attachment types and adult relationships
- Outline limitations of Hazan and Shaver's study
- Explain how psychological research relates to care of children, e.g. dealing with separation in nurseries, encouraging secure attachments through parenting classes, dealing with stranger anxiety in hospitalised children

Key terms

Here is a list of important terms that you should learn in your revision. Try to write definitions for these after reading the chapter, and check your answers in the glossary on pp. 129–135. Essential terms that you *must* know in order to properly understand the topic are marked with an asterisk.

Attachment bond*	Insecure-avoidant attachment*	Secure attachment*
Critical period*		Secure base
Deprivation*	Maternal deprivation*	Separation protest*
Insecure-ambivalent attachment*	Monotropy*	Stranger anxiety*
	Privation*	

Some important definitions

- **Attachment bond**: A long-enduring, emotionally meaningful tie to a particular individual (Schaffer, 1996).
- **Separation protest**: The distress that young children experience when they are separated from their primary caregiver.
- **Stranger anxiety**: The distress that young children experience when they are exposed to people who are unfamiliar to them.

Stages of attachment

Stages of attachment		
Stage	**Age**	**Response**
Asocial phase	0–6 weeks	Very young infants smile and cry but not at any special individuals
Stage of indiscriminate attachments	6 weeks to 7 months	From about 3 months, they smile more at familiar than unfamiliar faces
Stage of specific attachment – the first true attachment	7–9 months	Infants show two main signs that they formed a specific attachment to one person: • Stranger anxiety • Separation protest
Stage of multiple attachments	10 months onwards	Children begin to be attached to others. By 18 months, the majority of infants have formed multiple attachments

Individual differences: Insecure and secure attachment

The Strange Situation studies

Ainsworth investigated attachment behaviour using a set-up known as the "Strange Situation". This is a situation in which a mother and child are placed in an unfamiliar room containing interesting toys and observed through a one-way mirror. A series of episodes occurs (see table below). This method, in which behaviour is recorded in a very controlled setting, is known as a *controlled observation* (or structured observation).

The Strange Situation procedure	
Episode	**What happens**
1	The mother (or caregiver) takes the infant into the laboratory room
2	A stranger enters and approaches the baby with a toy
3	The mother leaves quietly If the child shows distress, the stranger offers comfort
4	The mother returns and greets the infant The stranger leaves The mother leaves again, waving bye bye
5	The baby is left alone
6	The stranger enters and interacts with the infant
7	The mother returns and picks up the child

The measures taken during the Strange Situation are given in the table below. Ainsworth found considerable differences in these measures between children and, on the basis of this, she classified attachment into three types.

Types of attachment			
Infant's behaviour	Secure attachment	Insecure-ambivalent	Insecure-avoidant
Willingness to explore and play with new toys	Infant happily explores the new toys	General signs of insecurity; does not explore the new toys with much confidence; stays close to mother	Plays with toys but with no particular enthusiasm
Stranger anxiety – the response of the child to the stranger	Child moves closer to mother but will carry on exploring the environment while keeping a wary eye on the stranger	Moves even closer to mother. Will not interact with the stranger	Shows little or no reaction to the stranger nor any preference for caregiver over stranger
Separation protest – the response of the child when the mother leaves	Considerable distress	Very distressed	Not very distressed, if at all
Reunion behaviour – how the child reacts when the mother returns	Delighted to see her; distress quickly disappears; cuddles contentedly with her	Shows signs of anxiety and anger	Shows little reaction
Notes	This is the optimal (best) form of attachment; mother is a secure base	Mother is not a secure base	Child shows no obvious signs of being attached

EVALUATION

➕ The Strange Situation studies look at an important aspect of human behaviour. Separations do happen in real life and it is important that we investigate their consequences.

➕ Studies are replicable and thus reliable. We are therefore able to generalise from the results.

➖ Studies lack ecological validity. The studies are done in an artificial environment and so may not reflect everyday behaviour.

➖ Not an appropriate (valid) way to assess attachment in all children. If children have been in regular daycare from an early age, they are used to separations and their apparent lack of concern when the mother leaves could just reflect independence and self-reliance, not insecurity.

Bowlby's theory of attachment

Bowlby's theory covers two aspects of attachment:

- The way in which children form attachment bonds and the nature of these bonds.
- What happens if these bonds are not formed properly, that is, the effects of deprivation and privation on a child.

How attachment bonds are formed

The main features of Bowlby's theory on how attachment bonds are formed are:

- Children have an *instinctive need* to attach to one person and they are biologically "pre-programmed" to make such an attachment.
- This attachment starts around 7–8 months of age and prevents the infant from crawling away into danger.
- The bond that a child develops with its main caregiver (often the mother) is a very special one, different from other bonds that a child develops. The tendency to bond with one main person is called **monotropy**.
- There is a **critical period**, from 7 months to 3 years, during which the baby is most likely to form this attachment bond. If it is not formed by the age of about 3 years it is unlikely to form at all and the child may never attach to anyone.
- The first attachment serves as an *internal working model*, which is the basis of our expectations and rules regarding relationships in later life.

The effects of deprivation and privation

Bowlby's theory of what happens if the bond is not formed properly is as follows.

Short-term effects

Robertson and Robertson suggested that when children are first separated from their mother or mother substitute they go through three stages of reaction, known as *the syndrome of distress*.

Stage 1: Protest	Child attempts to follow the mother, scream and do everything they can to recover her. The child will continue looking for her long after she has gone
Stage 2: Despair	Child will often sob but in a more "helpless" way, making far fewer attempts to find the mother. The child tends to show a distinct loss of hope.
Stage 3: Detachment	Child appears calm and even "settled". However, this apparent calm often masks underlying distress. The child appears to be emotionally "flat", not really responding very much to anything

Long-term effects

Bowlby's maternal deprivation hypothesis

Bowlby argued that if children do not have their need for attachment satisfactorily met, they may suffer from **maternal deprivation**.

■ **Maternal deprivation is said to occur when a child under the age of 3 years is deprived of his or her mother figure for a period of at least 3 months, or has a number of changes of mother figure.**

Bowlby argued that research, mainly in orphanages and hospitals, showed that maternal deprivation of this kind has the following effects:

- Emotionally disturbed behaviour such as bed-wetting.
- Dwarfism in children (not growing properly).
- Depression.
- Intellectual retardation.
- A crippling of the capacity to make relationships with other people – a so-called *affectionless psychopathy*.

Bowlby believed that there is a serious risk (around 25%) of the damage being *permanent* unless the situation can be reversed in the first 3 years of life.

The following study is one of several on which Bowlby's maternal deprivation hypothesis is based.

STUDY: 44 JUVENILE THIEVES: BOWLBY (1944)

Aim: To investigate the causes of delinquency in adolescence and assess whether it was related to separation in early life.

Method: From the clinic for disturbed adolescents where he worked, Bowlby selected two groups of boys:

- 44 juveniles who had a criminal record for theft.
- 44 adolescents with emotional problems who had never been in trouble with the law.

Bowlby interviewed them all to assess whether they showed signs of affectionless psychopathy. He also interviewed the families to see if the boys had had any significant separations from their main carers in the first 2 years of their lives. He studied the background and personality of the young thieves over 3 years.

Results: Bowlby found that 17 (39%) of the criminals had been separated from their mothers for 6 months or more before they were 5 years old. Of these, 14 (89%) appeared affectionless: they were cold and uncaring, felt no shame for what they had done and seemed quite detached from ordinary standards of decency. Of the second group, only two had been separated as children and only two appeared affectionless.

Conclusion: Bowlby concluded that one of the main causes of delinquent behaviour was separation of the child and mother (or main carer) in the first 5 years of life.

EVALUATION OF BOWLBY'S THEORY OF ATTACHMENT

➕ There is evidence from other species to support Bowlby's theory: Certain species (such as ground nesting birds) have evolved an attachment mechanism so that they are kept nurtured and safe.

➕ The theory has important applications. It has been fundamental in changing certain practices, such as encouraging parents to visit (or stay with) children in hospital and the abandonment of large-scale orphanages in favour of smaller homes or foster care.

➖ Not all evidence supports the concept of monotropy: Most children form attachments with more than one person and the quality is no less.

➕ There is some evidence to support the maternal deprivation hypothesis, including Bowlby's study of the 44 juvenile thieves (1944).

➖ There are problems with using the 44 thieves study as evidence for the long-term effects of separation: it only shows a *correlation* between separation and later personality problems; and it does not necessarily show cause and effect. It is quite possible that a third factor, such as a very stressful family life, had caused both the separations and the personality problems.

The distinction between privation and deprivation

Rutter (1972) conducted his own research into maternal deprivation. He agreed with certain aspects of Bowlby's maternal deprivation hypothesis but disagreed with others, and believed that it needed to be modified. Here are some of the important points he made:

- It is very important to distinguish between the effects of *never* forming a bond (as in the case of children raised in orphanages) and *breaking* a bond (i.e. being separated from the mother).

■ **Rutter used the term privation to describe a situation in which a bond is never formed and deprivation to describe the circumstances that occur if there are constant separations.**

- The failure to develop bonds with anyone (privation) in early childhood is the main factor in the development of affectionless psychopathy.
- It is family discord and the lack of a stable relationship with a parent that are associated with later antisocial behaviour, delinquency and criminal behaviour.

Behaviourist theory of attachment (the "cupboard love" theory)

The behaviourist theory sees the attachment bond as the result of learning rather than a natural instinct – it proposes that children attach to their main caregiver because this person provides enormous amounts of positive reinforcement. Positive reinforcers include:

- Feeding
- Attention
- Loving care
- Responsiveness

The last three are forms of social interaction and the fact that this is a powerful reinforcer implies that children are innately predisposed to enjoy the company of others and the comfort and attention they receive from them.

EVALUATION OF THE BEHAVIOURIST THEORY OF ATTACHMENT

➕ The theory is supported by the research of Schaffer and Emerson (1964), who found that infants most readily attach to those who are responsive to the infants' needs rather than those people who care for them most of the time. This supports the behaviourist view because it is these people who provide the most reinforcement.

➖ Attachment is an instinctual need rather than a learned preference. Even when children do not receive reinforcement from any individual, they make desperate attempts to try to form an attachment bond to someone. This implies that children have a need to attach, and that it is not simply the incidental result of reinforcement and something the child can easily do without.

- It is difficult for this theory to account for the suddenness with which certain reactions in the attachment process occur and, indeed, the reason for them. It is difficult, for example, to see why children suddenly develop stranger anxiety. This does not fit with a behaviourist approach because it occurs quite suddenly and without any unpleasant experiences being associated with unfamiliar individuals.

- It does not explain the emotional intensity that attachments involve; it seems doubtful that extremely strong emotions can depend simply on learning.

Types of love and attachment

Relationship between attachment types in infancy and romantic attachments in later life

Hazan and Shaver (1987, 1990) argue that the kinds of attachment bonds we form in childhood influence the style of loving we experience as an adult. Securely attached infants become securely attached adults, and so on. The following core study was used as support for this theory.

CORE STUDY: HAZAN AND SHAVER (1987)

Aim: To see if there is a relationship between attachment type and later experiences in romantic relationships.

Method: The researchers placed a "Love Quiz" in a local newspaper and analysed the replies of the 620 adults (aged 14–82 years) who responded. The quiz classified them as secure, insecure-avoidant or insecure-ambivalent in adult romantic relationships. They then answered questions about their relationship with their parents.

Findings: There was a correspondence between the relationship with parents and the relationship with their partner in adulthood:

- Those people who showed *secure attachment* in infancy were confident in their adult relationships.
- Those who were *avoidant* in infancy tended to become nervous when people got too close to them.
- Those who showed *ambivalent (anxious or insecure) attachment* in early childhood worried that their partners did not really love them.

There were very similar percentages of attachment styles in romantic relationships as in infant attachment (56% secure; 24% insecure-avoidant; 20% insecure-ambivalent).

Conclusion: The type of attachment people have in infancy predicts the type of romantic relationship people have in adult romantic relationships.

Limitations:

- The sample of adults used could have been biased and therefore not representative. They were all readers of one particular newspaper and chose to complete a "Love Quiz" in a newspaper.
- Data may not have been accurate because recall of childhood experiences may not have been reliable.
- The categorisation of adult romantic experiences into three broad categories is rather crude and may not reflect the subtleties of people's experiences.
- Correlational data: The relationship between infant attachment experiences and adult romantic relationships is only a correlation and therefore does not necessarily show that the childhood experiences *caused* the adult experiences, as suggested by the theory.

Application of research into attachment: Care of children

The research on attachment has had a significant effect on the way children are treated. It has helped to inform childcare practices in many walks of life, such as nurseries, hospitals and foster homes. In addition, it has given guidance as to how to help parents form secure attachments with their children. We will look at a small but important sample of these applications.

Dealing with separation in nurseries

It is important that parents and carers liaise closely to ensure that there is consistent care for each child and that any problems can be sorted out at an early stage:

- If the nursery is large, then each child should be looked after by the minimum number of people so they are not encountering strangers on a regular basis.
- Carers need to speak to children in a sensitive and caring manner.
- The nursery needs to be of good quality, with a low child-to-adult ratio, small numbers of children and a sensitive, stimulating and warm relationship between carers and children.

When the quality of care is good both at home and at the nursery, children should be able to develop secure attachments and develop well both socially and intellectually.

How to cope with children in hospital

Before

If the child is old enough and there is advance notice that they will be in hospital, prepare them by talking to them about what will happen. There are also books written especially for the purpose of describing to children what happens when people go to hospital. It is very important to tell them that they will return home (young children may think this is a permanent change of living arrangement).

During

- Regular visiting is obviously important and some parents may even be able to stay.
- Many hospitals now ensure that a child has a particular "special" nurse who is "their" nurse and whom they can become attached to. This is particularly important if the stay is a long one.
- For children whose parents cannot visit very often, there is a voluntary group of hospital visitors and, again, children are often given their "own" friend to visit them.
- Other contact with the home is important (e.g. regular phone calls and postcards).
- Constant reassurance that they will go home eventually is important.

After

When the child is back home, parents need to be tolerant of tantrums, upset sleep patterns, bed wetting, childish behaviour and such like. Children will take a while to resettle after a period away from home.

Encouraging secure attachments through parenting classes

Many people find parenting quite a challenging task. Parenting classes provide support and advice to parents on how to cope with children and ensure that they are well adjusted and happy – that they develop secure attachment bonds.

A typical course, entitled "Mothering on Solid Ground", offers the following advice and help:

- It reassures mothers that it is normal to feel physically, emotionally and/or mentally exhausted after childbirth and that this can lead to insecure attachments with their babies as well as other problems.
- It emphasises that, due to society's expectations, mothers feel that they should be able to be a good parent without any help or respite. It urges them to take any help offered and to seek it if necessary.
- It provides a great deal of practical help in managing toddler behaviour in such a way as to make parenting an enjoyable experience and the relationship between parent and child a secure and happy one.

• It tackles fundamental issues that can lead to unhappiness and insecurity, such as self-doubt, the disapproval of others and conflict between parents as to how children should be treated.

In conclusion, parenting classes do appear to help foster good relationships between parents and children. Since such relationships are the foundation of well-adjusted, happy children they are of great benefit to society as a whole.

OVER TO YOU

Now try the following revision activities:

1. Copy out the table on p. 27 showing the episodes in the Strange Situation studies. Cut out the different episodes, jumble them up and then put them back into the correct order.
2. Write the following words or phrases onto cards, with the definitions on the back:

   • **Monotropy**
   • **Critical period in attachment**
   • **Deprivation**
   • **Privation**
   • **Separation protest**
   • **Stranger anxiety**

   Now test yourself (or get a friend/family member to test you) by reading the word or phrase and then giving the definition.
3. Draw a storyboard to illustrate Hazan and Shaver's (1987) survey of the relationship between attachment types and adult relationships. Include at least two limitations.

EXAMPLE EXAM QUESTIONS

1 Pair up the types of attachment on the left with the behaviours shown in the Strange Situation on the right by drawing a line between them. **3 MARKS**

Secure attachment	**Infant does not show stranger anxiety nor is upset when the mother goes**
Insecure-ambivalent	**Infant is very upset when the mother leaves and is not readily comforted by her when she returns**
Insecure-avoidant	**The child uses the mother as a safe base**

2 Explain **two** criticisms of Bowlby's theory of attachment. **4 MARKS**

3 Outline the findings from Hazan and Shaver's (1987) study into types of attachment. **3 MARKS**

4 Explain how psychological research has helped parents and nursery staff cope with separation in pre-school nurseries. **4 MARKS**

MODEL ANSWER TO QUESTION 4

Psychological research shows that securely attached children can cope with time away from the main carer as long as this care is of good quality. It is important that nursery staff should be receptive to the child's needs and provide consistent and loving care with, as far as possible, one member of staff being the main carer for the child. A low child-to-staff ratio is best for the children in a nursery setting, with as little turnover of staff as possible. There should be a happy, stimulating environment in which the child feels secure and valued. There should be frequent communication between the parent(s) and the nursery staff so that any problems can be sorted out at an early stage.

SOCIAL PSYCHOLOGY: Obedience

5

What's it about?

Social psychology is about how we interact with other people when by ourselves or when in groups. These interactions help to shape who we are and how we act in subsequent similar and different situations. This helps us to perceive the world in a particular way. It also helps us to understand the world we live in. The area of focus for this broad topic in psychology is obedience and defiance – why are some people obedient and why are some people defiant? The factors that may stop people being obedient or change their obedience levels are also considered by social psychologists.

WHAT'S IN THIS UNIT?

The specification lists the following things that you will need to be able to do for the examination:

- Distinguish between obedience and defiance
- Explain what is meant by the term denial of responsibility
- Explain the effect of environment on obedience (setting, culture)
- Explain the effect of authority and the power to punish on obedience
- Explain the criticisms of situational factors as an explanation of obedience
- Consider dispositional factors as an alternative theory with specific reference to the role of the authoritarian personality in obedience
- Describe and outline limitations of the Bickman (1974) study
- Outline an application of research into obedience, e.g. keeping order in institutions

Key terms

Here is a list of important terms that you should learn in your revision. Try to write definitions for these after reading the chapter, and check your answers in the glossary on pp. 129–135. Essential terms that you *must* know in order to properly understand the topic are marked with an asterisk.

Anonymous	Debriefing	Informed consent
Authoritarian	Defiance*	Laboratory experiment
personality	Denial (or diffusion) of	Obedience*
Authority figure	responsibility*	Participants
Collectivist	Ecological validity	Protection of
Confederates	Extraneous variables	participants
Conformity	Individualistic	Right to withdraw

Some important definitions

- **Obedience:** When people behave in a certain way because they go along with the demands of an authority figure.
- **Defiance:** When people want to resist the demands of authority and not do as they are told.
- **Denial (or diffusion) of responsibility:** When people feel less answerable for their behaviour because there are other people around. Any "responsibility" is shared, so no individual feels responsible.

The effect of authority and the power to punish

This can be explained via the study of Milgram (see pp.16–20 of *Psychology for GCSE Level, 2nd Edition*).

STUDY: MILGRAM (1963)

Aim: He wanted to test out "destructive obedience" in a laboratory.

Method: Milgram advertised for participants. Forty participants were then used in the study. Each participant met a Mr Wallace (a confederate) thinking that he was also a participant in the study. However, it was always "fixed" that the participant was the teacher whilst Mr Wallace was the learner. After this, Mr Wallace was seen being strapped into an "electric chair" device in the next room. The participant then left to sit in front of the "shock generator" in the next room. He was told that he would read out a series of word pairs (e.g. blue box). After reading out the pairs, he was instructed to read just one word.

The participant was instructed that if Mr Wallace got one of them wrong they were to give him an electric shock via the "shock generator". The first button was for 15 volts and then every button increased the shock by 15 volts. The first incorrect answer would therefore get 15 volts. This continued until the participant reached 450 volts! If the participant said that they did not want to continue then the experimenter had to verbally "prod" them. When the participant had given Mr Wallace the 300-volt shock, Mr Wallace would hit the wall repeatedly so that the participant could hear it. From that point on, Mr Wallace did not answer another word-pair task.

Results: All of the participants gave a minimum of 300 volts to Mr Wallace, and 65% gave 450 volts despite the button having XXX above it. Some continued to give 450 volts repeatedly, as Mr Wallace's silence meant a wrong answer!

Conclusion: The study clearly demonstrated that people do show high levels of obedience to an authority figure when they are allowed to punish someone for getting a task wrong.

EVALUATION

- It was a laboratory-based study, so Milgram could be confident that the situation the participants were placed in directly affected the shocks given by the participants.

- It lacks **ecological validity**. That is, the task may not represent whether we would be obedient in a real-life situation.

- Many psychologists criticise Milgram on ethical grounds. They believe that he did not get informed consent (nowhere on the advertisement does it state the true aim), was deceitful, did not allow them the right to withdraw and placed all of the participants under high levels of psychological stress.

- However, he did follow up the participants to make sure that they were all fine months after participating. Virtually all of the participants were pleased to have taken part in the experiment.

The effect of environment on obedience

See p. 25 of *Psychology for GCSE Level, 2nd Edition*.

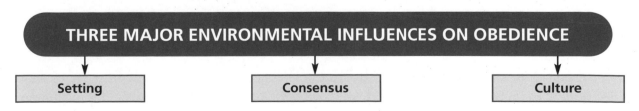

THREE MAJOR ENVIRONMENTAL INFLUENCES ON OBEDIENCE

Setting	Consensus	Culture

Setting

Milgram's experiments that looked at the status of the authority figure included:

- *Ordinary man.* In this study Milgram chose to have an ordinary man as the person giving the orders (authority figure). He was dressed in normal clothes (so no white laboratory coat!)
- *Run-down building.* In this study Milgram changed the setting. He chose to run the experiment in a run-down commercial building in a shopping area.

Condition	Participants who gave 450 volts	Participants who gave 300 volts	Mean voltage given by the participants
Original	65.0%	100.0%	405 V
Ordinary man	20.5%	30.0%	240 V
Run-down building*	47.5%	62.5%	300 V

*It should be noted that here two participants refused to give even the lowest shock of 15 volts. This is the only variation on Milgram's experiment where some participants gave no shock whatsoever.

Consensus

Note that in this variation both Teachers 1 and 2 are confederates. The real participant is Teacher 3.

1. At 150 volts, Teacher 1 refuses to go any further with the experiment. The authority figure (the experimenter) insists they continue but this teacher sits in another part of the room. The real participant is then given the job of reading out the word pairs as well as giving out the electric shocks.
2. At 210 volts, Teacher 2 now refuses to go any further. The authority figure yet again insists they continue but the teacher sits elsewhere in the room, stating "I'm willing to answer any of your questions, but I'm not willing to shock that man against his will. I'll have no part of it."

Voltage	150 volts	210 volts	450 volts
Number of participants who stopped	4	21	4
NB: 62.5% of the sample refused to break the consensus view of *not* going to the very end.			

Culture

Kagitcibasi (1996) examined parental attitudes to their children's behaviours across a wide range of nationalities. In certain countries, such as Turkey and Indonesia, it was expected that children were obedient to their parents with little room for independence. However, other countries such as USA and Korea were the opposite: independence was encouraged and obedience discouraged.

Replications of Milgram

Country	Participants who went to 450 volts
Australia	68%
Italy	80%
Austria	85%

Finally, some psychologists will use the individualistic–collectivist argument for obedience – cultures that are **individualistic** are theoretically less likely to be obedient than **collectivist** cultures.

Criticisms of situational factors as an explanation of obedience

- One of the main criticisms of research that has assessed the role of situational (environmental) factors is that they are not real situations being tested out.
- Other variables may be causing obedience, such as the dispositional (e.g. personality) factors of that person. See the next section for an explanation.

Dispositional factors and obedience

See p. 27 of *Psychology for GCSE Level, 2nd Edition*.

Authoritarian personality

- According to Adorno, a person with this type of personality is intolerant of others with differing views, is dominating, is attracted to groups where there are strong leaders and respects higher authority figures.
- Adorno stated that an authoritarian personality is formed by having parents who are strict, cold and expect obedience in their child.

- As a result, the child becomes obedient later in life (or expects others to be obedient to them).
- One way in which people can be assessed for this type of personality is to complete the F-scale that was created by Adorno. The person reads a range of statements and has to state how much they agree with each statement.

CORE STUDY: BICKMAN (1974)

See pp. 27–28 of *Psychology for GCSE Level, 2nd Edition*, for more detail.

Aim: To investigate the social power of a uniform.

Method: Participants were the 153 pedestrians in a street in New York. All pedestrians were always alone.

The type of authority figure was varied:

1. The authority figure wore a sports jacket and tie.
2. The authority figure wore a milkman's outfit.
3. The authority figure wore a uniform that appeared to be that of a policeman.

Also, the type of situation was varied:

1. Picking up a bag scenario.
2. Dime and meter scenario.
3. Bus stop "no standing" scenario.

Results: See graph below.

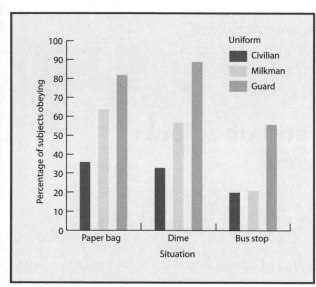

Conclusion: Bickman could conclude that a uniform has the power to make people obey simple demands such as picking up a bag, lending a dime to a stranger or moving at a bus stop!

Limitations:

- The small sample sizes in each of the conditions could be criticised as not being large enough to make generalisations to other pedestrians.
- Also, as the study was a field experiment, there are many variables that Bickman could not have controlled for. For example, some of the participants may have been late for an important meeting and therefore did not help.

- The sample was predominantly white so it may be difficult to generalise to other races, especially as all of the experimenters were white.

Obedience can be related to the amount of perceived authority.

Application of research into obedience

See pp. 48–49 of *Psychology for GCSE Level, 2nd Edition.*

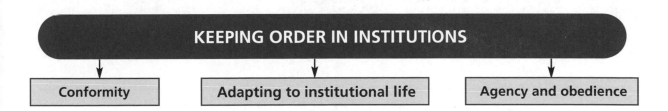

Conformity

The idea of normative conformity can be applied to prisons. Inmates may conform to the prison system because of a desire to be liked.

Adapting to institutional life (Goffman, 1961)

There are three phases:

- In the *colonisation* phase, prisoners make themselves fully at home in the prison and do not want to leave. As a result, prisoners will go along with the demands of the prison for this to happen.
- In the *conversion* phase, the prisoner imitates the actions of staff and is used by them on various tasks. Therefore, when a prisoner is in this phase he will follow the rules of the prison without question.
- Finally, in the *playing it cool* phase, prisoners may not be fully cooperative with rules and regulations but will follow them sufficiently to survive their stay in prison.

Agency and obedience

Milgram proposed that for a prisoner to do this they must have two social states:

1. *An autonomous state*: This is when we are free to act as we wish.
2. *An agentic state*: This is when we give up our free will in order to serve the interests of a wider group.

OVER TO YOU

Now try the following revision activities:

1. Create a spider diagram *or* mind map for the sections on the effects of the environment on obedience and keeping order in institutions. Make sure you draw little pictures to remind yourself of the material.
2. Type up the Bickman study into short sentences that cover the aim, all of the procedure, all of the results and then the conclusion. Cut out each sentence and muddle them all up. Then, place them back in the correct order.

EXAMPLE EXAM QUESTIONS

1 Distinguish between obedience and defiance, making sure you use an example in your answer. **3 MARKS**

2 Outline **one** way in which the environment may affect obedience. **3 MARKS**

3 Outline **one** criticism of situational factors as an explanation of obedience. **3 MARKS**

4 Outline **two** limitations of the Bickman (1974) study. **4 MARKS**

MODEL ANSWER TO QUESTION 4

One limitation of this study is the sample size – not the overall size but the number per condition. There were about 17 in each condition, which means that it may be difficult to generalise the findings to the rest of the general public. A second limitation is that it was a field experiment. This means that certain variables could not be controlled, which may have affected obedience. For example, a person may not have helped that day if they felt ill but would normally help out when feeling well.

6

INDIVIDUAL DIFFERENCES:
Atypical Behaviour

What's it about?

Most of psychology is concerned with looking for "laws" of behaviour that can be applied to everyone irrespective of culture, upbringing, etc. Behavioural (or learning) psychologists are interested in ways in which the environment we live in affects our behaviour. Therefore, they examine ways in which we can *condition* behaviour in animals and humans using things such as learning by association. As a result, if we learn this way then we can *un*-learn behaviours in the same way! The area of focus here is how we develop phobias and then how we can help people to overcome them.

WHAT'S IN THIS UNIT?

The specification lists the following things that you will need to be able to do for the examination:

- Distinguish between typical and atypical fear
- Outline common types of phobia: agoraphobia, social phobia, school phobia, acrophobia and arachnophobia
- Distinguish between an unconditioned stimulus, a neutral stimulus and a conditioned stimulus
- Distinguish between an unconditioned response and a conditioned response
- Use the process of classical conditioning to explain the onset of phobias
- Explain the criticisms of the behaviourist theory of atypical behaviour
- Consider evolutionary theory as an alternative theory with specific reference to preparedness
- Describe and outline the limitations of the Watson and Rayner (1920) study
- Apply research into atypical behaviour, e.g. behaviour therapy

Key terms

Here is a list of important terms that you should learn in your revision. Try to write definitions for these after reading the chapter, and check your answers in the glossary on pp. 129–135. Essential terms that you *must* know in order to properly understand the topic are marked with an asterisk.

Association	Genetics	Social learning
Aversion therapy	Neutral stimulus*	Systematic desensitisation
Classical conditioning	Phobia	Unconditioned stimulus*
Conditioned stimulus*	Preparedness	
Flooding	Role model	

Some important definitions

- **Conditioned stimulus**: What the neutral stimulus turns into after conditioning. It produces a learned conditioned response.
- **Neutral stimulus**: A stimulus that causes no response.
- **Unconditioned stimulus**: A stimulus that elicits an involuntary bodily response (one that is usually biological and is not learned).

Typical and atypical behaviour in relation to fear

- Typical fears are ones that makes evolutionary sense as they represent a dangerous situation (e.g. feeling fear on top of a high building).
- Atypical fears are ones that do not make sense at all. Is being fearful of baked beans or cotton wool dangerous?

Common types of phobia

A **phobia** is defined as an irrational fear of something, someone or some object:

- *Agoraphobia*: Fear of open spaces and/or public areas.
- *Social phobia*: Fear of being in social situations.
- *School phobia*: Fear of going to school.
- *Acrophobia*: Fear of heights.
- *Arachnophobia*: Fear of spiders.

Classical conditioning

Classical conditioning is all about learning through **association**.

An example

Pavlov already knew that dogs salivate when they smell meat powder. Every time the powder was given to the dogs he sounded a metronome (a device that clicks at set intervals). He repeated this a few times. Then he sounded the metronome *without* the meat powder and noticed that each dog still salivated.

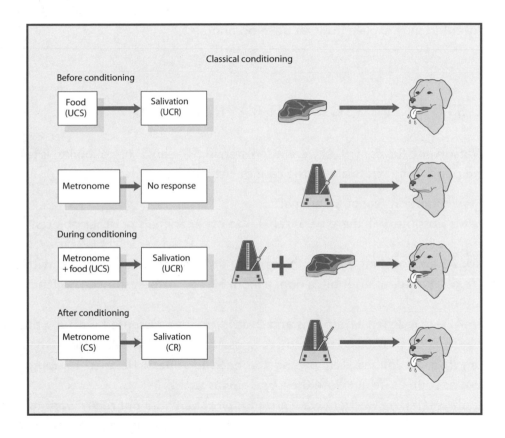

Other important terms linked to classical conditioning

- *Generalisation*: This occurs when we produce a conditioned response to a stimulus that is *similar* but not the same as the conditioned stimulus.

- *Extinction*: This occurs when the conditioned stimulus no longer produces the conditioned response.
- *Spontaneous recovery*: This occurs after extinction. Suddenly, in the presence of the conditioned stimulus, the conditioned response reappears!
- *Discrimination*: This occurs when we produce a conditioned response to only *one* specific stimulus even if there are similar ones in the environment. So you may show a fear of wasps but not bees.

Classical conditioning and the onset of phobias

A classic study in psychology conducted by Watson and Rayner (1920) can help us to show how classical conditioning may explain how we develop phobias.

CORE STUDY: WATSON AND RAYNER (1920)

Aim: Watson and Rayner (1920) were interested in two aims. The following is taken directly from the paper they wrote about the case of Little Albert:

1. Can we condition fear of an animal?
2. If that is possible, will there be a transfer to other animals or other objects?

Method: At approximately 9 months of age, Little Albert was presented with a range of stimuli (e.g. a white rat, a rabbit, a dog, a monkey, etc.). Albert showed no fear towards any of the objects.

When Albert reached 11 months and 3 days, he was presented with a white rat again and, as before, he showed no fear. However, as Albert reached out to touch the rat, Watson struck an iron bar immediately behind the head of Albert! He tried to approach the rat again but as soon as he got close the iron bar was struck.

Seven days later, he was very wary around the rat and did not really want to play with it or touch it. When he did reach out the loud noise was made, the same as the previous week. This was done five times during the session. Finally, the rat was presented by itself and Albert began to cry and crawled away rapidly.

Results: Over the next month Albert's reactions to a range of objects were observed. He was still fearful of the white rat. He showed negative reactions to a rabbit being placed in front of him and a fur coat (made from seal). He did not really like cotton wool but the shock was not the same as it was with the rabbit or fur coat. He even began to fear a Santa Claus mask!

Limitations:

- As it was basically a case study, it could be difficult to generalise to a wider population.
- As the procedure was highly controlled in nature, it may *not* explain how we acquire phobias in everyday life. Therefore, the study lacks ecological validity.
- The study has been deemed unethical as Albert was not *deconditioned* – that is, they never got rid of Albert's phobia at the end of the study.

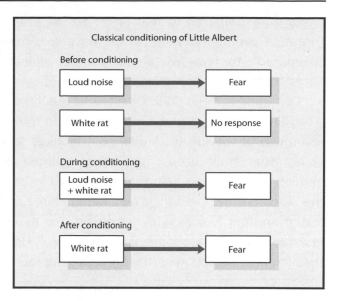

Criticisms of the behaviourist theory of atypical behaviour

Social learning

If we use the four principles of Attention, Retention, Reproduction and Motivation we can see how social learning theory can also explain the development of phobias:

- *Attention* – Mummy draws attention to herself by screaming loudly and running around.
- *Retention* – Especially if mummy is rarely seen running around and screaming loudly, the child will retain this event in their memory.
- *Reproduction* – Remember how a person has to be *capable* of reproducing the behaviour for it to be truly socially learnt. Well, the child can also run around and scream loudly.
- *Motivation* – The child must be motivated to reproduce the behaviour. The child saw the consequence of mummy's actions: the spider is disposed of and she gets a cuddle!

However, social learning is not very good at explaining why we become scared of objects or things that we have never encountered.

Evolutionary explanation of phobias

Preparedness

Could it be that we are pre-programmed to fear certain objects that may be potentially harmful? That is, there are certain objects or things that we are *expected* to be frightened of so we are *biologically prepared* to fear them! So, we fear objects and things that might be of a survival threat in evolutionary terms. We have fear-relevant stimuli such as snakes that we may be "prepared" to fear. We also have fear-irrelevant stimuli such as flowers that we are *not* "prepared" to fear.

Cook and Mineka (1989) wanted to see if monkeys could become phobic of objects such as a crocodile, a flower, a snake or a rabbit even though they had never seen them before. Using the technique of splicing the video, each monkey saw the same rhesus monkey being scared of the object that their group had been assigned. So, for example, one monkey saw another monkey on the video being scared of the crocodile. The next monkey saw the same monkey on the video but this time they were being scared by the flower! And so on. Each monkey was then tested on their fear towards the object. The monkeys in the crocodile and snake groups showed fear towards a toy crocodile and a toy snake. However, when the other two groups were shown their "feared object" (e.g. the flower or the rabbit), they did *not* show any fear.

Genetics

This takes the idea of **preparedness** further by saying that certain phobias are encoded into our genetic make-up (DNA) and passed down through generations.

Ost *et al.* (1991) reported that 64% of patients with a blood and/or injection phobia had at least one first-degree relative (immediate family) with the same phobia. In the general population, 3–4% are phobic of blood and/or needles.

Fredrikson, Annas and Wik (1997) examined 158 phobic females who were scared of snakes or spiders and discovered that 37% of mothers and 7% of fathers also had the same phobia!

However, Fredrikson asked the participants another question: whether direct exposure to the phobic stimulus (e.g. they had been frightened by the phobic object directly) or indirect exposure to the phobic stimulus (e.g. seeing someone else being phobic towards the object) had happened. The indirect exposure was the most common for snakes (45%) than for spiders (27%). So, even though it looked like the phobia was caused by genetics, nearly half of the snake-phobic participants could have their phobia explained via **social learning**.

Behaviour therapy

Systematic desensitisation

Systematic desensitisation works on the idea that the phobia can be *unlearnt*. The end point should recondition the patient so that the conditioned stimulus (which will be the phobic stimulus) produces a conditioned response of relaxation rather than fear.

The principles

- The patient is taught relaxation skills so that they understand what it feels like to have relaxed muscles.
- The patient produces an anxiety or fear hierarchy to work through with the therapist.
- You can only work through the hierarchy of fear once each stage has been successfully completed, whereby the patient is showing signs of relaxation in the presence of the specific thing in the fear hierarchy.

You can see from the diagram that in the conditioning phase there are competing responses of fear and relaxation. This is called *reciprocal inhibition*, whereby it is impossible to experience both emotions at the same time.

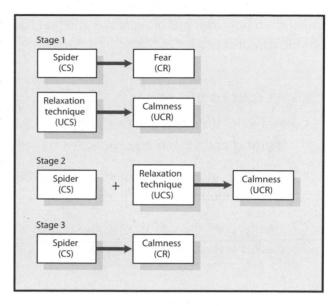

EVALUATION

⊕ Capafons, Sosa and Avero (1998) reported that their 20 patients with a fear of flying who had several sessions working through their anxiety hierarchy became much less fearful of flying after the study ended.

⊕ Zettle (2003) showed that systematic desensitisation can be applied to people who fear maths. Anxiety decreased markedly for those who completed their systematic desensitisation, even though their maths ability never changed!

⊕ Ventis, Higbee and Murdock (2001) found that relaxation techniques and simply laughing at the phobic stimulus were both effective in reducing fear in arachnophobics!

⊖ There is a lack of follow-up studies to see if the patient is still cured of their phobia.

⊖ Some psychologists believe that even though you work slowly through a hierarchy of fear, you are still being unethical by making people confront their phobias.

Flooding

The patient is exposed to the largest anxiety-provoking stimulus straight away (usually direct contact with the stimulus; this is called *in vivo*). Obviously, the patient is going to feel extreme levels of fear but this dies off quite rapidly because the body cannot sustain such a high level of arousal for a long time. The patient quickly learns that there is now nothing to be fearful of! The association between phobic stimulus and fear has been broken, to form a new relationship of the phobic stimulus producing calm.

EVALUATION

⊖ Many psychologists believe that this therapy is *unethical* as it causes distress, both physiologically and psychologically, to the patient.

⊕ However, other psychologists would argue that the end outcome of curing the phobic fear is enough to justify the high distress caused in the short term.

⊖ Finally, even though this technique is used by psychologists, there have been hardly any studies testing its effectiveness.

Aversion therapy

- It follows the principle of associating a noxious stimulus (something horrid) with an already conditioned stimulus to produce a different conditioned response.
- Therefore, after repeated "new" associations, the unwanted behaviour (conditioned stimulus) decreases as it is now associated with something noxious.
- Aversion therapy has been used on alcoholics, to "cure" people of homosexuality or to treat sex offenders such as paedophiles.

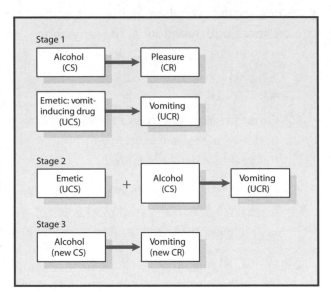

EVALUATION

⊖ A great number of psychologists believe that aversion therapy for homosexuals is highly unethical. Who has the right to change someone else's behaviour just because they consider it to be "abnormal" or "atypical"?

⊕ If the aversion therapy is combined with some social skills training it has been shown repeatedly to be effective for paedophiles (Davison & Neale, 1998).

✪ Even though the behaviour that needs to be changed is not totally eliminated, it provides the patient with a greater control over that behaviour (Monaghy, 1994).

✪ Cautela (1966) reported that *covert sensitisation* as a form of aversion therapy is effective. The patient has to simply imagine unpleasant circumstances (e.g. a cocaine addict pictures himself just beginning to snort and then straight away visualises being violently ill).

OVER TO YOU

Now try the following revision activities:

1. Buy some index cards and write the words *unconditioned stimulus*, *unconditioned response*, *conditioned stimulus*, *conditioned response* and *neutral stimulus* on separate cards. On the reverse of each, write what they were for in the Pavlov study. Then you can attempt to place them in the correct order; turn them over and see if you are correct. You could do the same for Little Albert (see p. 261 of *Psychology for GCSE Level, 2nd Edition*).
2. Create a series of mind maps – one for each theory that you may be asked questions about in the examination. Ensure you use lots of colours to help the information stick into your memory.

EXAMPLE EXAM QUESTIONS

1 Name and describe **two** phobias you are familiar with. **2 MARKS**

2 Outline **one** way in which we can acquire a phobia. **5 MARKS**

3 How can the case of Little Albert be explained by classical conditioning? **5 MARKS**

4 Distinguish between an unconditioned stimulus and a conditioned stimulus. **3 MARKS**

MODEL ANSWER TO QUESTION 4

An unconditioned stimulus is an unlearned (natural) stimulus that produces a natural response – e.g. with Pavlov, food (the unconditioned stimulus) naturally produces salivation in the dogs. However, a conditioned stimulus is one that is learned. It is what the neutral stimulus turns into once it has been paired with the unconditioned stimulus a number of times. An unconditioned stimulus is natural, whereas a conditioned stimulus is learned.

BIOLOGICAL PSYCHOLOGY: Criminal Behaviour

7

What's it about?

Crime fascinates people and arouses strong emotion. In both fact and fantasy it is a very important part of our everyday lives. In this chapter we start by considering how society decides which particular behaviour should be considered criminal and then look at the biological causes of crime and the alternative view put forward by social learning theory. Finally we will consider how psychological research can be applied to criminal behaviour by looking at ways in which crime can be reduced.

WHAT'S IN THIS UNIT?

The specification lists the following things that you will need to be able to do for the examination:

- Outline the problems of defining and measuring crime
- Explain the concept of a criminal personality
- Explain the role of heritability in criminal behaviour
- Explain the role of brain dysfunction in criminal behaviour
- Describe the facial features associated with criminals
- Explain the criticisms of the biological theory of criminal behaviour
- Consider social learning theory as an alternative theory
- Describe Mednick et al.'s (1984) adoption study into the genetic basis of criminal behaviour
- Outline limitations of Mednick et al.'s study
- Explain how psychological research relates to crime reduction

Key terms

Here is a list of important terms that you should learn in your revision. Try to write definitions for these after reading the chapter, and check your answers in the glossary on pp. 129–135. Essential terms that you *must* know in order to properly understand the topic are marked with an asterisk.

Behaviour modification	**Family studies**	**Vicarious punishment**
Brain dysfunction	**Heritability***	**Vicarious reinforcement***
Consensus view	**Morality**	
Crime*	**Token economy**	

The problems of defining and measuring crime

The definition of a **crime** is anything that is forbidden by the criminal justice system.

Ways of deciding what is criminal

- **The consensus view:** Actions are considered to be crimes if most people within the group agree that they should be (consensus means agreement).
- **The morality view:** Morals are beliefs and values that are used by society to judge what is right or wrong. The morals held by a society influence what is classed as criminal. However, immorality and criminality are not the same thing. This means that not everything that is considered morally wrong is illegal (such as telling lies), nor is everything illegal necessarily immoral (it's illegal to park on a double yellow line but it is not immoral). Nevertheless, morality is the basis of much of our law making.

Problems of defining crime

There are many problems with deciding what should constitute a criminal act. The following are a few important ones:

- *There is not always agreement*: Within any society there is bound to be disagreement about what should constitute a crime, so there are campaigners who argue for certain actions to be made criminal and others to be decriminalised.

- *People have different moral values*: If morality is used as a basis for making behaviour criminal, then parliament has to decide whose moral values will be used as the basis for deciding what constitutes a crime. Indeed, some philosophers argue that morality alone should never be the basis for deciding what constitutes a crime.
- *Values change over time*: Societies change their minds about what is criminal, partly due to changes in attitudes (homosexuality was a crime in England up until 1967) and partly because there are new technologies (such as cars and computers) that bring new possibilities for cheating or harming others. One of the most recent serious crimes to appear in the statute book in many countries concerns sexual abuse using the internet.
- *Different societies have different values*: Although there are some behaviours that are considered criminal in all societies, other actions are criminal in some societies and not in others (e.g. adultery is criminal in some but not most societies).

Problems of measuring crime

There are two main ways in which crime is measured:

1. By records kept by the police and criminal justice system.
2. By large-scale surveys carried out for the government.

Records kept by the police (and criminal justice agencies)

The Home Office produces a publication called *Criminal Statistics* that provides a record of crimes in England and Wales and also provides information on who the victims and criminals are. There are two main reasons why this information is limited or even misleading:

1. The number of crimes, rather than the number of criminals, is recorded so we have no accurate record of the number of criminals.
2. It greatly underestimates the number of crimes committed because a large number of crimes go unreported. There are several reasons for this, including the following:
   - Some crimes are not considered serious enough by the victim for them to be reported to the police.
   - Sometimes the victim is too scared to report it (e.g. sexual abuse).
   - Some crimes, such as fraud, are not detected.
   - Some people do not choose to deal with the police, so would only report a crime if it was really serious.
   - Sometimes the police do not report the crime.

Information from surveys

The biggest survey in Britain is the *British Crime Survey*, which is carried out every 2 years. Thousands of people aged 18 years or over are interviewed about any crimes, however petty, that they have been the victim of over the last year. The purpose is to compare this with the number of crimes reported in *Criminal Statistics* so as to get a more accurate view. However, this can also be inaccurate for several reasons, including the following:

- People may have forgotten, especially if the crimes were carried out more than a year ago.
- People may be too embarrassed to say.
- People may choose not to tell the truth.
- Some crimes, such as shoplifting, are not detected.
- The survey only takes account of household and personal crime, so crimes such as company fraud or shoplifting would not be included.

You can see, therefore, that crime statistics are inaccurate and can only ever provide a rough guide to the actual number of crimes committed.

Explanations of criminal behaviour

Biological theories

A criminal face? The work of Lombroso

Lombroso (1876) suggested that criminals were a kind of genetic "throwback" or savage with certain physical deformities that showed in their facial features (one of Lombroso's 1876 drawings is shown here). These features include:

- A narrow sloping brow (indicating that they were unintelligent).
- A prominent jaw (indicating that they had strong passions beyond their control).
- Drooping eyes.
- Twisted, flattish nose.
- High cheekbones.
- Large ears.

Lombroso later revised his original ideas to say that these types of people only accounted for about a third of all criminals and that the environment did play a part in making people criminal. Nevertheless, he still believed that a substantial minority of offenders were "born criminals".

Criminal tendencies are inherited

The extent to which characteristics are inherited is known as **heritability** and investigations of families help us to establish whether or not certain characteristics are inherited. There is support and criticism of the view that criminal behaviour is inheritable:

Support

- Osborn et al. (1979) found that about 40% of sons of criminal fathers were criminal themselves, as compared with 13% of sons of non-criminals.
- Hutchings and Mednick (1975) looked at criminality in both biological and adoptive fathers. They found that if only the biological father had a criminal record, 21% of their sons did, whereas if only the adoptive father had a criminal record, 11.5% of their sons did. This indicates that genetics are influential.
- See the core study below: Mednick et al. (1984).

Criticism

- The fact that there is a positive correlation (relationship) between the criminality of fathers and the criminality of their sons does not necessarily mean that genes are responsible for the criminal behaviour. It could be due to social learning, or a third factor such as the particular neighbourhood may be responsible.
- The adoptive family did have some influence. Both environment (the adoptive family) and genetics influence the likelihood of a boy becoming criminal.

CORE STUDY: MEDNICK ET AL. (1984)

Aim: To compare the rates of criminal conviction of the biological parents and the adoptive parents of a group of adoptees.

Method: The researchers investigated every adoption in Denmark between 1924 and 1947, which was nearly 14,500 people. They looked at:

- The number of criminal convictions they had.
- The number of criminal convictions their biological parents had.
- The number of criminal convictions their adoptive parents had.

They compared the criminal convictions of the adopted "children" (now adults) with the number of convictions of their biological and adoptive parents.

Results: The adoptees whose biological parents were persistent offenders were more likely to be arrested repeatedly as adults than those whose biological parents had clean records.

The percentage of crimes committed by the adoptees was higher if both their biological and their adoptive parents were criminals.

Conclusion: The researchers concluded that genetic factors did contribute to criminal behaviour. However, they did not believe they were the only cause, as demonstrated by the fact that the likelihood of children being criminal was increased if both their adoptive and biological parents were criminal.

Limitations:

[Notice that the limitations centre around problems concerned with the conclusion that genes are the main influence on criminal behaviour.]

- *There was no account taken of the neighbourhood in which the adopted children grew up.* If they grew up in a similar environment to their biological parents then it is possible that environment rather than genetics was responsible for their behaviour.
- *No account taken of social learning from biological parents.* Some of the adopted children may have spent some time with their biological parents in early life and this could have influenced them.
- *Self-fulfilling prophecy.* If the family who adopted the children knew they came from a criminal family, they may have treated them in a way that increased the likelihood of them becoming criminal. See p. 155 of *Psychology for GCSE Level, 2nd Edition*, for elaboration.
- *Children may have been influenced by adoptive parents.* It is possible that some of the adoptive parents had a criminal record before adopting children but kept this hidden.

Brain dysfunction

It is possible that brain dysfunction may account for some criminal behaviour. Brain dysfunction (damage) may be the result of problems the individual had from birth or the result of accident or disease later in life.

This theory is supported by Raine et al. (1997), who compared murderers who were pleading guilty by reason of insanity with murderers who made no such plea (the controls). They found that, compared to the controls, there was less activity in the prefrontal cortex of the brain of the "guilty by reason of insanity" group. This area is linked to self-control. They also found differences in the amygdala, which is one of the structures in the brain that helps to control violent behaviour.

Of course this study only looks at a relatively small number of people who have committed one type of crime (and who are pleading insanity), so the findings do not generalise to all types of crime or even to all murderers.

Criticisms of the biological theory of criminal behaviour

- *It does not take account of environmental factors*. Factors such as socialisation and culture have a strong influence on behaviour. Socialisation involves the way you are brought up within the family and the values you are given. The culture and subculture also provide values, which in turn influence behaviour. Biological theories do not take sufficient account of these.
- *The studies supporting the biological approach have serious limitations*. Walters (1992) has analysed a fairly large number of family studies (including adoption studies) and found a small relationship between crime and genes but a greater one between environment and crime. He points out that some of the older studies were quite poorly designed.

Social learning theory and crime

Social learning theory offers a different way of looking at the causes of crime. This can be summarised by the following points:

- Children learn by *observation* and *imitation*.
- They copy the behaviour of *role models* such as parents, same-sex peers (friends), older same-sex siblings and the media.
- One of the factors that makes behaviour more likely to be imitated is if the role models are seen to be reinforced (rewarded) for their behaviour. The process of being indirectly reinforced is known as **vicarious reinforcement**. Thus, if criminal and/or violent behaviour is seen to be rewarded, then children are likely to copy it.
- Children also copy acts that they themselves are *directly* rewarded for. When crimes are committed one of the main reinforcers is material gain, but there are other powerful reinforcers, including admiration, attention and respect.
- This theory easily accounts for why crime may run in families. The children of criminals see a powerful role model (their father or, less often, their mother) commit a crime and copy it, especially if the parent is a respected or feared member of the local community who is obeyed by others.

Application of research into criminal behaviour: Crime reduction

Biological means

If crime is biological in origin, then there is little that can be done to reduce crime or prevent it other than sterilise criminals (so they cannot produce children) or imprison them for life. In modern society this is not considered desirable or necessary.

Imprisonment

This is one way of coping with crime. Prisons serve a variety of purposes:

- They *punish* criminals by depriving them of their liberty.
- They *deter* the criminals themselves and others from re-offending.
- They *prevent* the criminals from re-offending while they are in prison.
- They provide *rehabilitation* – education, training and treatment to restore offenders to a useful life on the "outside".

Token economy programme: A type of behaviour modification

This works on a fairly simple basis of rewarding good behaviour. Every time a prisoner (or young offender) shows desirable behaviour, such as cooperation or doing as they're told, they are given a token. Tokens can be collected and exchanged for rewards such as leisure activities, sweets and passes home. The system is quite successful at controlling behaviour within the institution but whether it improves behaviour in the long term in the outside world is less certain.

Short sharp shock

A system based very much on punishment rather than rewards is a "short sharp shock" regime for young offenders based on the belief that a short, highly unpleasant custodial sentence will "shock" young offenders and deter them from committing future crimes. A Home Office Report in 1984 reported that these regimes were no better or worse than any other regime at influencing behaviour once the offenders were released, and the same applies in the USA. See p. 158 of *Psychology for GCSE Level, 2nd Edition*, for a discussion of this.

Relationship to theory

Imprisonment, the token economy and the short sharp shock are all related to *learning theory*, specifically to *operant conditioning*. Imprisonment and short sharp shock are designed to work on the principle that punishment reduces the likelihood of re-offending. The token economy system works on the concept of positive reinforcement: that offering reinforcement increases the likelihood that desirable behaviour will be repeated.

OVER TO YOU

Now try the following revision activities:

1. On one side of a card write the following and then answer them briefly on the back. Use them as revision aids.
   • A definition of crime.
   • Two ways of deciding what is criminal.
   • Two ways in which crime is measured.
   • Three biological theories of crime.
   • What is "heritability"?
   • The main principle of social learning theory.
   • The procedure of the study by Mednick et al. (1984).
   • The main principles of a token economy system.
2. Draw a mind map to illustrate the biological theories of crime. Most of these theories lend themselves well to drawings that represent the main points, so illustrate these but add the support/criticisms in words.

EXAMPLE EXAM QUESTIONS

1 Outline **two** problems of measuring crime. **4 MARKS**

2 Explain the role of brain dysfunction in criminal behaviour. **4 MARKS**

3 Explain how psychological research relates to crime reduction. **10 MARKS**

MODEL ANSWER TO QUESTION 1

One problem with measuring crime is that many crimes are not reported by the public. There are several reasons for this. Some crimes may be seen as too petty to report (e.g. a stolen purse that only contains a small amount of cash) or the probability of catching the criminal is too small. Some serious crimes, such as rape, may not be reported because the victim is reluctant to go to court due to the trauma that this involves.

Another problem of measuring crime is that many crimes probably go undetected. For example, much shoplifting is undetected and there are almost certainly incidents of fraud that are never known about, especially petty fraud.

COGNITIVE PSYCHOLOGY: Perception

8

What's it about?

Cognitive psychology is the study of how the mind works and how it can influence our behaviour and experiences of the world. This type of psychologist is interested in mental processes such as attention, memory and perception. Is it that our experiences of the world make us perceive things in a particular way, or are we born with the ability to understand the world around us straight away? This is one debate that cognitive psychologists are interested in.

WHAT'S IN THIS UNIT?

The specification lists the following things that you will need to be able to do for the examination:

- Describe the difference between sensation and perception using shape constancy, colour constancy and visual illusions
- Explain depth cues, including linear perspective, height in plane, relative size, superimposition and texture gradient
- Outline the role of experience in perception
- Explain the concept of top-down processing
- Explain the concept of perceptual set
- Explain the criticisms of the constructivist theory of perception
- Consider the nativist theory as an alternative theory, with specific reference to bottom-up processing in perception
- Describe and outline limitations of the Haber and Levin (2001) study
- Outline an application of research into perception, e.g. advertising

Key terms

Here is a list of important terms that you should learn in your revision. Try to write definitions for these after reading the chapter, and check your answers in the glossary on pp. 129–135. Essential terms that you *must* know in order to properly understand the topic are marked with an asterisk.

Bottom-up processing	Linear perspective	Relative size*
Colour constancy*	Nativist theory	Sensation*
Constructivist theory of perception	Nature–nurture debate	Shape constancy*
Convergence	Perception*	Superimposition*
Depth cues*	Perceptual set	Texture gradient*
Height in plane*	Readjustment studies	Top-down processing
		Visual illusion*

Differences between sensation and perception

- **Sensation** refers to when we are sensing the environment around us using touch, taste, smell, sight and sound (the senses).
- **Perception** is about making sense and using the information we have stored via our senses.

Shape constancy, colour constancy and visual illusions

Shape

Shape constancy refers to our ability to understand that objects remain the same basic shape even when viewed from a variety of angles.

Colour

Colour constancy refers to our ability to understand that objects remain the same colour even when viewed in differing levels of light.

Illusions

The Müller-Lyer illusion

In the illusion below, which of the blue lines is longer, the one on the left or the one on the right?

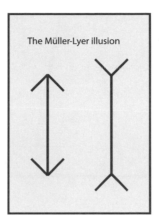

Of course, the answer is that they are the same length! So, why are we "tricked" into believing that the one on the right is longer?

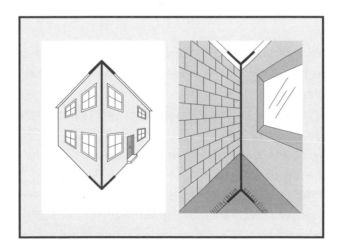

It's all about our perception of distance and depth. In the figure above, the blue line on the left is the outside of a building going away and hence gives the perception of being smaller as it is "going away from our eyes". The blue line on the right is the corner of an inside room so the perception is that it is coming towards you and getting larger. Hence the right-hand line is perceived to be larger.

The Ponzo illusion

Which of the two blue rectangles is longer, A or B?

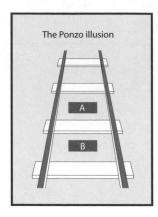

Of course, both are of the same length! The two lines either side of A and B are converging into the distance, hence we perceive that the picture is going further away and are tricked into believing that A is longer.

Depth cues

- *Linear perspective*. With a railway line the tracks run in parallel, but when we look at the train tracks into the distance they seem to get closer and closer the further away they get from our eyes. This is called convergence.
- *Texture gradient*. The fineness in detail decreases the further away the object is from the eye.
- *Superimposition*. If one object hides part of another object, then the object that is still "complete" is perceived to be closer.
- *Height in plane*. This follows the "rule" that the closer an object is to the horizon, the further away it is compared to other objects seen in the same picture or scene.
- *Relative size*. An object's smaller size on your retina when it is further away from you is called its **relative size**.

Which depth cues are present in the figures on the opposite page?

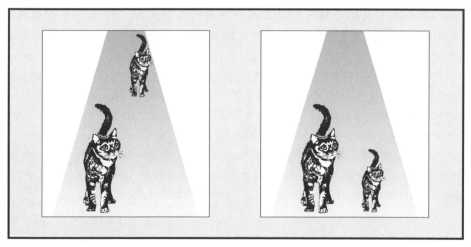

See pp. 241–243 of *Psychology for GCSE Level, 2nd Edition*, for more examples of depth cues.

Role of experience in perception

Nurture and perceptual abilities

STUDY 1 (MAN–ELEPHANT–ANTELOPE): HUDSON (1960)

Aim: To test out the depth-perceptual abilities in two-dimensional pictures of a varied group of people living in the southern regions of Africa.

Method: 562 participants were shown a variety of pictures of the same hunting scene but with differing depth cues. They were shown a series of six pictures (see p. 244 of *Psychology for GCSE Level, 2nd Edition*) and asked the following questions:

1. What do you see?
2. What is the man doing?
3. Which is nearer, the man, the elephant or the antelope?

Results: For picture 1 (elephant on hill behind antelope), about 34% of the participants responded with "antelope" to question 3, indicative of 3D perception. In pictures 2 and 3 (superimposition), 51% of participants responded with correct 3D perception to *all* questions in *both* pictures.

Conclusion: Hudson believes that this shows perception to be learned from our cultural experiences. If 3D perception was nature (in this case, inherited), then all participants should have shown that ability.

A further study that reported cultural differences was reported by Segall, Campbell and Herskovits (1963). They showed the Müller-Lyer illusion (shown on p. 71 of this chapter) to 15 different cultures, ranging from Europeans to a variety of African peoples. The Europeans were much more likely to be tricked (around 16%), whereas some of the African peoples had scores as low as 1.7%. Segall tried to explain the differences in terms of the *actual* explanation of how the Müller-Lyer illusion works (see p. 240 of *Psychology for GCSE Level, 2nd Edition*, for more detailed explanation). Europeans are used to a highly carpentered environment. Segall believed that many African people have not had this experience.

Readjustment studies are also useful in the nature–nurture debate. If our world is changed (e.g. by wearing goggles to make us see the world upside down) and we can adapt to it without making mistakes, then it shows that perceptual abilities are learned.

STUDY 2 (GOGGLES): KOHLER (1962)

Aim: To review some of the literature on "experiments using goggles" that change the way we see the world.

Method: Two such studies were by Erismann in Austria and Gibson in America. Erismann, for example, got his participants to wear goggles that inverted the world from left to right or from top to bottom. Another device allowed the participant to only see the world as a "rear view".

Results: Generally, participants adapted to their new view of the world. For one participant, after several weeks of wearing goggles that inverted left to right, he had got so used to it that he could ride his motorcycle through a city whilst wearing the goggles!

Conclusion: Some psychologists believe this is evidence that we *learn* how to perceive the world. If it was due to nature then no one would have been able to perform the tasks.

Top-down processing

Top-down processing of information – your past experiences, thoughts and expectations – affects your perception. This could affect you consciously or unconsciously.

An example

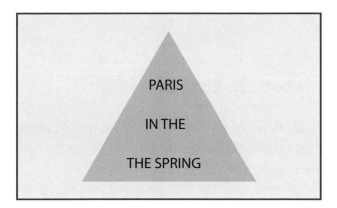

Perceptual set

A perceptual set refers to a readiness or a predisposition to perceive things in a specific way. This is affected by previous experiences and expectations of what could be perceived.

An example

With the rat–man picture, if you had been looking at pictures of rats beforehand it is predicted that you are much more likely to see the rat.

Criticism of the constructivist theory of perception

We can criticise the whole idea of the constructivist theory by simply stating that it ignores the role of our inborn abilities. We can still try to perceive objects, pictures, etc. that we have never come across before in order to make sense of the world. The constructivist theory would predict that we could never make sense of anything novel as we have no prior experience to draw upon.

The next section on *nativist theory and bottom-up processing* can be used as evidence against the constructivist approach.

Nativist theory and bottom-up processing

The *nativist theory* of perception predicts that we are born with many perceptual capabilities. We simply use them, when we need them, even if we have to wait until adulthood. Therefore, perception is encoded in our genetic make-up.

Bottom-up processing refers to the idea that when information arrives from our senses it sets a pattern recognition process into motion. The combination of these simple data allows us then to perceive more complex patterns.

Nature and perceptual abilities

STUDY 1 (VISUAL CLIFF): GIBSON AND WALK (1960)

Aim: To test whether infants have depth perception.

Method: Gibson and Walk created a visual cliff. There were 36 infants used in the study, ranging from 6 months to 14 months. Each child was tested individually. They were placed near the centre of the apparatus and their behaviour was recorded.

Results: Of the infants who moved when placed on the visual cliff, 27 crawled towards the shallow side. Only three crawled over the cliff side. The remainder did not move at all.

Conclusion: Some psychologists believe this shows that depth perception already exists in human infants because the majority of infants instantly crawled onto the shallow side. However, some psychologists would argue that, because the infants were aged between 6 and 14 months, it may not all be nature as they could have *experienced* some depth perception before being placed on the visual cliff.

Gibson and Walk's visual cliff

STUDY 2 (DEPRIVATION): GREGORY AND WALLACE (1963)

Aim: Gregory and Wallace wanted to investigate the perceptual abilities of a man who had been blind for 50 years but then had his sight restored.

Method: SB became blind at 10 months. At the age of 50 years he had a corneal graft to restore his sight. About 48 days after his final operation, the first tests and observations began.

Results: He was initially questioned about whether he had any visual memories before becoming blind. He could only remember what the colours red, white and black looked like. When Gregory first observed SB walking down a corridor he did it with "ease", even guiding himself through a doorway without the use of touch. It was difficult to spot that he had only just had his sight restored after 50 years!

However, there were some differences compared to a normal sighted person. SB would never look around the room and would only focus on objects when specifically asked. His estimates of lots of things were nearly accurate. For example, he was surprised by the height of a bus but not its length. He found traffic very frightening and would not cross a road without assistance, even though when blind he was very confident with this behaviour.

Conclusion: Some psychologists believe this shows that our perceptual system is with us from birth but others say it was 48 days before SB was tested so he may have "learned" things before the test.

CORE STUDY: HABER AND LEVIN (2001)

Aim: To investigate whether size perception and distance perception are independent in our perceptual system.

Method:

- *Study 1*: In this study 109 male university students were presented with the names of 50 common objects. Some were token *invariant* (easy to predict size) and some were token *variable* (a potentially wide range of sizes). The participants were simply asked to estimate the height of each object listed, in feet and inches.
- *Study 2*: Nine male college students (volunteers) were used because they had normal or corrected-to-normal vision. They were given 45 stimuli to look at (15 token invariant, 15 token variable and 15 geometric shapes of different colours). The setting was a large grassy field as drawn out below:

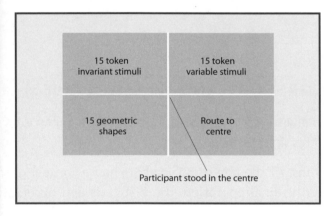

All the participants (in groups of three) were required to do was to estimate the distance from the centre to the object, and then estimate the object's size.

Results:

- *Study 1*: The students could accurately gauge the size of the 50 objects. The accuracy of judgements was significantly better for token-invariant objects.
- *Study 2*: As with the first study, estimates of size of object were largely accurate. Participants were equally accurate compared to the participants in Study 1 at estimating the size of objects. Participants could also quite accurately estimate the sizes of the unfamiliar geometric shapes!

Conclusion: Haber and Levin concluded that because the participants were quite accurate under all conditions, distance and size perception are skills that work independently in humans. That is, participants could accurately estimate size irrespective of distance and they could also accurately estimate distance irrespective of size of object.

Limitations:

- The sample consisted of males only, so generalising these findings to how females use size and depth perception might be difficult.
- As this sample was American, the results may be culturally specific. There is no way of knowing if other cultures' perceptual systems are the same as in this sample.
- There is also an assumption that the 50 common objects were seen as common by the entire sample – experiences with the objects pre-study may be dramatically different.

An application of research into perception: Advertising

Karremans (2006) tested out whether *subliminally* projecting a branded drink (Lipton Ice) to a group of participants would subsequently affect their choice of drink. Those who were subliminally primed did choose Lipton Ice more often. The control group showed no preference.

Key (1973) also showed that when the phrase U Buy was embedded backwards (so at some point the word Yubu appeared) in a presentation advertisement for alcohol, 80% of participants chose the U Buy rum after they had watched the advertisement. In addition, Byrne (1959) highlighted that it is probably only single words or two-word phrases that can be perceived subliminally and then affect behaviour.

Williams et al. (2005) tested out whether we could pick up on emotions subliminally. Participants were shown faces representing fear either subliminally (16.7 ms) or *supraliminally* (500 ms, so you would actually see the face – this is the term psychologists use for this type of processing). Different parts of the brain were used when processing subliminally and supraliminally, but there was much more processing happening in the latter group.

OVER TO YOU

Now try the following revision activities:

1. Type up the Haber and Levin study into short sentences that cover the aim, all of the method, all of the results and then the conclusion. Cut out each sentence and muddle them all up. Then, place them back in the correct order.
2. There are many definitions to learn for this topic. Get some index cards and write the term on one side of the card and its definition on the other side. Then, get someone to test you on your definitions. You could also give an example of each definition by drawing a picture to explain each term. Alternatively, you could draw an example of each definition and get another person who is sitting the exam to tell you which term it is.

EXAMPLE EXAM QUESTIONS

1 Define the following terms using an example:

(a) Relative size. **2 MARKS**

(b) Bottom-up processing. **2 MARKS**

2 Outline **one** piece of evidence that supports the role of experience in perceptual abilities. **5 MARKS**

3 Using an example, explain what psychologists mean by the term *perceptual set*. **3 MARKS**

4 Outline the results of the Haber and Levin (2001) study into perception and evaluate it in terms of **two** limitations. **6 MARKS**

MODEL ANSWER TO QUESTION 3

This is when we are predisposed to perceive something in a particular way. It is based on our previous experiences with similar stimuli. These can be experiences in the distant or immediate past and can be seen with ambiguous drawings and pictures. There is one called the duck–rabbit illusion. If a person is exposed to pictures of ducks before looking at it, they are more likely to see the duck rather than the rabbit.

DEVELOPMENTAL PSYCHOLOGY: Cognitive Development

9

What's it about?

People used to think that the main difference between children and adults was that children knew less than adults. However, we now recognise that this is not true; children actually think differently from the way in which adults think. In this chapter we will look at the work of one of the most important developmental psychologists, Piaget, who studied a great many children and developed a theory to describe the way in which children's thinking changes as they grow older. We will then look at an alternative approach, that of Vygotsky. Finally, we will consider how Piaget's and Vygotsky's theories have been applied to education.

WHAT'S IN THIS UNIT?

The specification lists the following things that you will need to be able to do for the examination:

- Describe how cognitive development occurs in invariant and universal stages.
- Outline the stages of cognitive development: sensorimotor, pre-operational, concrete operational and formal operational.
- Describe the concept of object permanence
- Describe the concept of egocentrism and the process of decentring
- Describe the concept of conservation
- Explain the criticisms of Piaget's theory of cognitive development
- Consider Vygotsky's theory as an alternative theory, with specific reference to the zone of proximal development
- Describe Piaget's (1952) experiment into the conservation of number
- Outline the limitations of Piaget's study
- Explain how psychological research relates to educating children

Key terms

Here is a list of important terms that you should learn in your revision. Try to write definitions for these after reading the chapter, and check your answers in the glossary on pp. 129–135. Essential terms that you *must* know in order to properly understand the topic are marked with an asterisk.

Active/discovery learning*	Egocentrism*	Scaffolding*
Clinical interview	Formal operational stage*	Sensorimotor stage*
Concrete operational stage*	Object permanence*	Symbolic thought
Conservation*	Pre-operational stage*	Zone of proximal
Decentre*	Reversibility	development*

Piaget's theory

Piaget believed that as children get older they go through several stages of thinking.

The sensorimotor stage (birth to 2 years)

- Children learn via their senses (touch, taste, hearing, sight) and through actions (grasping, sucking).
- They live in the "here and now".
- They lack **object permanence**, that is, if they cannot see an object, it does not exist. The lack of object permanence begins to disappear at around 10 months but does not disappear fully until the end of this stage.

During the sensorimotor stage, infants lack object permanence. If an object is seen to be placed in one location, but then retrieved from another, this would elicit surprise.

The pre-operational stage (2–7 years)

The main achievement is **symbolic thought**, which is the ability to use one concept to represent another. This is shown in several ways, the most important of which are:

- Language (a word represents a concept).
- Pretend play (e.g. playing games such as mummies and daddies).
- The ability to understand ideas of past and future.

Limitations of the pre-operational stage

- **Egocentrism** – the inability to see things from another's point of view, as demonstrated by the "three mountains" study.
- **Lack of conservation skills** – the inability to understand that things remain the same even when their appearance changes. The inability for younger children to conserve was demonstrated by a series of experiments illustrated in the Piaget core study.

We will now look at these two studies in turn.

STUDY: THE THREE MOUNTAINS STUDY: PIAGET AND INHELDER (1956)

Aim: To see if children in the pre-operational stage (under about 7 years old) are egocentric and unable to view things from another person's point of view.

Method: A model showing three mountains was placed on a table. These mountains were different colours, with snow on top of one, a house on another and a cross on the third. A doll was placed on one side. The child was asked to say *what the doll could see* by choosing one of 10 pictures.

Findings: The 4-year-olds always chose a picture that matched how they themselves saw the model. Most children under 7 years old could not choose the correct model.

Conclusion: Egocentrism is a characteristic of the pre-operational stage.

CORE STUDY: PIAGET (1952)

Aim: To see if children of various ages can conserve number.

Method: Two identical rows of counters are laid out on a table. Once the child has agreed that they are the same, the adult spreads out the counters in one of the rows (as illustrated below) and then asks the child if the rows contain the same number of counters.

● ● ● ● ● ● ●   ● ● ● ● ● ● ●
● ● ● ● ● ● ●   ● ● ● ● ● ● ●

Findings: Children in the pre-operational stage will usually say that there are more counters in the longer row.

Conclusions: Younger children fail to conserve because they base their judgement on appearances.

Limitations:

- *Possible misunderstanding in language.* It is possible that young children's failure in the task may be caused by the fact that they do not really understand "more than" or "less than" rather than not understanding conservation.

- *The children may not understand what is expected of them and become confused.* The children were asked the same question twice (are the same numbers of counters in each row?) and may assume that a different answer is required the second time around.
- *Assumptions may be made because the adult deliberately moved the counters.* Younger children may have thought that because a grown-up had rearranged the counters it was fair to assume that something must have changed. They were less likely to think this if a "naughty teddy" rearranged the counters.

The core study investigated *conservation of number* but there are other types of conservation, including:

- Volume (liquid).
- Substance (solid quantity, such as amount of modelling clay).
- Area.

Children in the pre-operational stage assume that what they themselves see is the way the world is. They cannot **decentre** – step outside their own viewpoint and see things from another's point of view.

The concrete operational stage (7–11 years)

Achievements

- Children now begin to perform *logical operations*: for example, they now understand that if nothing is added or taken away then things must remain the same, despite appearances. This means they can now conserve.

- They are no longer entirely egocentric and can now understand things from a variety of angles and viewpoints.

Limitation

They can only manage logical thinking if concepts are presented in a "concrete" way, that is, by the use of familiar objects. *They cannot deal with abstract concepts or hypothetical tasks.* In order to solve problems, a child needs to be able to refer to real objects.

The formal operational stage (11 years +)

Achievements

- Adolescents can now deal with hypothetical situations – they can move beyond the *actual* states of the world and think of the *possible* ones.
- They can solve problems in a systematic, logical manner in which all possible combinations of factors are considered.

These abilities are shown by the pendulum task (see p. 199 of *Psychology for GCSE Level, 2nd Edition*).

Summary of Piaget's stages	
Sensorimotor	• Learning through senses and action • Lives in the here and now • Full object permanence lacking
Pre-operational	• Has symbolic thought • Egocentrism • Inability to conserve
Concrete operational	• Can perform operations with familiar material • No longer egocentric • Can conserve • Cannot deal with abstract concepts or hypothetical tasks
Formal operational	• Can deal with hypothetical concepts • Can solve problems in a systematic, logical way

The nature of cognitive development

It is important to note two aspects of the stages of cognitive development:

- They are *invariant*: This means that they are always in the same order and none of the stages can be skipped because each successive stage builds on the previous stage and represents a more complex way of thinking.
- They are *universal*: This means that they apply to all children the world over, regardless of culture.

Criticisms of Piaget's theory

Underestimation

Several studies (such as Hughes' "Policeman doll" and McGarrigle and Donaldson's "Naughty teddy" studies below) question the findings of Piaget's studies. They indicate that it is possible that he underestimated the abilities of young children, especially in terms of egocentrism and conservation of number.

STUDY: THE POLICEMAN DOLL: HUGHES (1975)

Aim: To see if young children can see things from another's point of view when faced with a familiar task.

Method: Each child in turn sat at a table on which was placed an arrangement of four walls set at right angles to one another to form a cross (see picture). A policeman doll was put at the end of one wall so it could "see" into the two sections divided by the wall. The child was then asked to put a boy doll in a place where the policeman couldn't see him.

Results: 90% of children aged $3\frac{1}{2}$ –5 years could cope with this task.

Conclusion: Children may not be as egocentric as Piaget imagined.

STUDY: THE NAUGHTY TEDDY: McGARRIGLE AND DONALDSON (1974)

Aim: To test children's ability to conserve using the standard method that Piaget used and a variation in which a naughty teddy is used to rearrange the counters.

Method: In the *control condition* children were given conservation tasks identical to those used by Piaget and using the same procedure. In the *experimental condition* the same tasks were used, but this time a glove puppet called Naughty Teddy rearranged the counters.

Results: When Naughty Teddy rearranged the row, 62% of 6-year-olds thought there was the same number of counters, whereas in the control condition only 16% of this age group thought there was still the same number.

Overestimation

Some research shows that many adults never reach the formal operational stage, especially on scientific reasoning problems (King, 1985). Piaget was aware of this and argued that most people attain some kind of formal operational thinking but can only apply it to certain specialised areas with which they are very familiar. For example, a car mechanic may use formal operations to work out how to repair a car but not in other areas such as discussing philosophical questions.

Criticisms from Vygotsky

(*See Vygotsky's theory on the next page.*)

- Underestimation of importance of culture.
- Too much emphasis on children making progress if they discover things for themselves and not enough on the role of experienced adults in helping children learn.

The methodology used by Piaget

- In writing about the sensorimotor stage, Piaget used a small number of children and his observations were not checked. This has been criticised because researchers should not make generalisations based on only a few people or when their observations have not been checked by other people.

- Piaget used clinical interviews when asking children questions. A clinical interview is an unstructured interview, the purpose of which is to gain insight into the individual's thought processes. A problem with a clinical interview is that children may be led by the researchers into certain answers.

Vygotsky's theory

- *The importance of culture*: Vygotsky proposed that cultures teach people *how* to think as well as *what* to think. He believed that each culture provides its children with the *tools of intellectual adaptation* that permit them to use their mental functions more adaptively. For example, in Western culture we teach children to write things down and take notes in order to organise information and help them to remember it, whereas other cultures may show children how to carry out adult tasks.
- *The role of others*: A major theme of Vygotsky's theory is that *social interaction plays a fundamental role in the development of understanding of the world*. He believed that children learn more if they work with people who are more experienced than they are and that they make little progress if left to explore the world alone. This is linked to the next concept.
- *The **zone of proximal development***: This is defined as the area between the level of performance a child can achieve when working alone and a higher level of performance that is possible when working under the guidance of more skilled adults or peers. The fundamental idea is that there is a range of skills that children cannot do alone, but which can be developed with adult guidance or help from more experienced children. Equally, there is a limit to what a child can do, even with adult help. Cognitive development, then, is limited to a certain range at any given age, and full cognitive development requires social interaction.
- *Scaffolding*: This is defined as the appropriate support framework for children's learning. It is provided by adults (especially parents and teachers) and more experienced peers and is necessary for children to be able to learn for themselves and eventually internalise the concepts. Children eventually develop the problem-solving techniques that they have used with those of greater experience and then use them on their own. In this way, new cognitive skills are learnt.

Applying the theories to education

Applying Piaget to education

The main principles involved in applying Piaget's theory to educational practice can be summarised as follows:

- *Children must discover for themselves*: Children are innately curious and are pre-programmed to acquire and organise knowledge. Piaget believed that attempting to directly teach ideas and concepts could be harmful to cognitive development because it prevents children from discovering for themselves. Teachers should prepare tasks that are challenging yet achievable for the individual child and leave them to solve the tasks themselves.
- *Children are **active learners***: The role of the teacher should be to encourage the child to be active and to provide opportunities that foster their natural capacity to learn.
- *Children must be cognitively ready*: You cannot move a child from one stage to another if they are not capable of understanding the necessary concepts. The teacher needs to prepare lessons that encourage curiosity and challenge the child's current understanding, thus forcing them to re-evaluate what they already know. If the concepts are too complicated students will not be able to understand them, so no new learning will occur.
- *Teachers need to take account of individual differences*: Since children mature at different rates, they are better working in small groups on activities specially designed for their state of readiness.

Applying Vygotsky to education

- *Scaffolding is very important in educating children*: Youngsters do best if given help from adults or older peers who gradually allow them to do more and more of a task as their understanding increases.
- *The zone of proximal development*: This can be used as a guide to provide what the child needs in order to progress and learn at the maximum possible rate.
- *Students should be given every opportunity to experience the "real world"*: Schools should not be isolated places where children learn concepts that they never apply to real life.

OVER TO YOU

Now try the following revision activities:

1. Use a mnemonic to learn the stages in Piaget's theories: S, P, C, F. Make up a silly sentence or phrase with these as first letters so that it helps you remember them in the exam.
2. Write the name of each stage on a separate card and, using the table on p. 85, write the main characteristics of each stage on the back.
3. Summarise the main concepts of Vygotsky's theory (use the headings in the text, with a single sentence to describe each one).
4. Plan an answer to a question on how to apply Piaget's and Vygotsky's theories to education.

EXAMPLE EXAM QUESTIONS

1 Name the four main stages of Piaget's theory of cognitive development and outline **one** characteristic of each stage. **8 MARKS**

2 Explain how both Piaget's and Vygotsky's theories are related to educating children. **10 MARKS**

3 Penny is fed up because she thinks her mum has given her sister Kate more juice than she has been given. Mum points out to her that they each had the same size carton of juice to start with, but when she poured it into their new Christmas glasses, her sister's looked more because her Reindeer glass is taller and thinner than Penny's Snowman one. Penny is still cross and hides Kate's new glass in a cupboard, but Kate was watching and recovers it. Mummy tells her off for upsetting Kate but Penny does not understand why Kate is upset. Using the stimulus material where appropriate, answer the following questions:

   (a) Describe what is meant by object permanence. **2 MARKS**

   (b) Identify an example of object permanence. **1 MARK**

   (c) Describe what is meant by conservation. **2 MARKS**

   (d) Identify an example of lack of conservation. **1 MARK**

   (e) Describe what is meant by egocentrism. **2 MARKS**

   (f) Identify an example of egocentrism. **1 MARK**

MODEL ANSWER TO QUESTION 3

(a) Object permanence is the ability to understand that an object continues to exist even when it is out of sight.

(b) Kate looks for the glass when it has been hidden.

(c) Conservation is the ability to understand that changing the form of a substance does not change its amount. [Note that this question asks you to define conservation, not lack of conservation, but the next question asks about lack of conservation.]

(d) Penny thinks Kate has more juice than she has even when she knows that the juice was poured from the same size carton.

(e) Egocentrism is the inability to see things from anyone else's point of view.

(f) Penny does not understand why Kate is upset with her.

SOCIAL PSYCHOLOGY: Non-Verbal Communication

10

What's it about?

Communication is essential to survival. In humans it is a very important part of their social behaviour and they spend a great deal of time communicating with each other. An essential means of communication between people is verbal, that is, it involves speech and can also involve writing since this stands for language. But an additional and very important means of communicating is not by what we say but what we do. Even during speech, a great deal of information is conveyed by the *way* in which we speak. The tone of our voice, the gestures we use and our facial expressions all convey meaning. In this chapter we look at some of the non-verbal means by which we communicate, such as eye contact, facial expression and body language. We will then consider the extent to which these means of communication, so important for survival, are learnt by observation and imitation and therefore are more biological in origin.

WHAT'S IN THIS UNIT?

The specification lists the following things that you will need to be able to do for the examination:

- Outline examples of body language and facial expressions as a form of non-verbal communication (NVC)
- Explain the role of observation and imitation, and the role of reinforcement and punishment in learning NVC
- Describe cultural variations in NVC
- Explain criticisms of social learning theory of NVC
- Consider evolutionary theory as an alternative theory, with specific reference to survival and reproduction
- Describe Yuki et al.'s (2007) experiment into cross-cultural differences in interpreting facial expressions, and outline its limitations
- Explain how psychological research relates to social skills training, e.g. rehabilitation of criminals, customer-service training, managing conflict by managing body language

Key terms

Here is a list of important terms that you should learn in your revision. Try to write definitions for these after reading the chapter, and check your answers in the glossary on pp. 129–135. Essential terms that you *must* know in order to properly understand the topic are marked with an asterisk.

Body language*	Facial expression	Social learning theory*
Evolutionary theory	Non-verbal communication*	Verbal communication*
Eye contact	Postural echo	

Non-verbal communication

Definitions

- **Verbal communication** is communication that involves speech or is in written form.
- **Non-verbal communication (NVC)** involves messages expressed by communication other than linguistic means, that is, communication that does not use words. This includes the expression in the voice, gestures and body language.

Non-verbal communication can be divided into two types:

1. Communication during speech, such as the tone of voice, the pausing, the "hums and haws" and the general pace of the speech.
2. Communication that does not involve any speech at all, such as our posture or facial expression.

Body language

Posture

Posture is the way in which we walk, stand or sit (i.e. the way we hold our body) and is an important means of NVC. The following table gives examples of this means of communication.

Posture	Meaning
Hunched shoulders with head down	Lack of confidence
Shoulders back with head held high	Self-confidence; authority
Relaxed posture	"At home" feeling; lack of anxiety
Orientation of body towards a person, especially if leaning forward	Interest in the person
Leaning back from a person	Lack of interest in the person, or rather shy or reserved
Back straight with chest out: "puffing up"	Aggression and/or high status

Open and closed posture

The table above shows the meaning of various body postures. In general, we can describe postures as "open" or "closed":

Open and closed body postures

- An open posture is one in which we can see the body (the torso), with arms and legs uncrossed and shoulders back. This can convey one of several messages: self-confidence, a relaxed non-defensive state or even an aggressive one.
- A closed position is one that closes up the body by a more stooped posture with arms across the body, or arms folded and legs crossed if sitting down. It is a very defensive posture and shows a lack of self-confidence or nervousness.

Postural echo

This refers to the tendency of two people, when sitting together, to adopt postures that are the mirror-image of each other. For example, one person may cross their legs from right to left whilst the other crosses them left to right. As one leans forward, so does the other. They may even synchronise hand positions and hair grooming. It tends to demonstrate that the two people are getting along well and are "on the same wavelength".

Gestures

Gestures also provide a means of communicating in a non-verbal way. You will be familiar with the following gestures and their meaning:

Two friends exhibiting postural echo

Some everyday gestures and their meaning	
Beckoning finger	Come here
Shaking of fist	I'm very angry
Wave of arm	Goodbye
Wave of both arms	Pay attention to me/I'm over here
Shake of head	No
Nod of head	I agree
Shrug of shoulders	I don't know

Facial expression

Our facial expression conveys a wealth of meaning. Ekman et al. (1976) demonstrated that it is *innate* for people to recognise and be able to express the following emotions by facial expression:

- Surprise
- Fear
- Anger
- Disgust
- Happiness
- Sadness

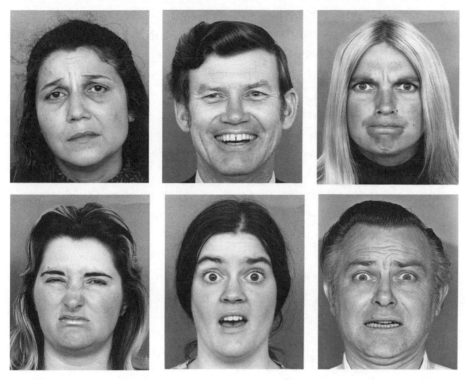

Copyright © Paul Ekman

The development of understanding of facial expression	
3–5 months old	Infants can discriminate first joy and then surprise, fear and sadness
2 years old	Children can recognise all six main facial expressions for emotion
6 years old	Children begin to recognise when the face and inner emotion do not match. In other words, they can tell that a sad person who is smiling is not really happy

Eye contact

Eye contact is a very basic way of communicating and is important from birth. There are many functions of eye contact, including the following:

1. *It provides feedback to others on our mood and personality*:
   - Moods: A high level of eye contact or gaze implies interest, intimacy, attraction or respect. A low level indicates embarrassment, shame or disinterest.
   - Personality: People who make frequent eye contact are judged as honest, straightforward, friendly and likeable (Kleinke et al., 1974). People who avoid eye contact are seen as unfriendly, shifty or shy (Zimbardo, 1977). See p. 103 of *Psychology for GCSE Level, 2nd Edition*.

2. *It regulates the flow of conversation*:
   - When we have a conversation with someone we look at them intermittently: we make eye contact in bursts of about 3 seconds and then look away.
   - Turn taking: Eye contact helps to show when the talker wants to carry on speaking and when they want to stop. People tend to look more at the end of what we are saying but look away at the start, especially if they are answering a question (Kendon, 1967).
   - Feedback: At the beginning of what they are saying people do not need a response, but towards the end of it they use eye contact to see how the conversation has been received.
3. *It expresses emotion*:
   - Pupil dilation expresses excitement, interest or fear. Hess et al. (1960) measured the pupil size of men and women whilst they viewed certain pictures and found that men's pupils enlarged by about 18% when they viewed a picture of a naked woman, whilst a woman's pupils enlarged by about 20% when she saw an image of a naked man. Subconsciously we take in this information and are affected by it – without a word being said, people know if someone is interested in them and they respond accordingly.

Social learning theory as an explanation for NVC

The role of imitation and observation

- Children and adults often learn by *observing* and then *imitating* the behaviour of other people.
- The people who are imitated are referred to as *models*. The most important models in a child's life are firstly their parents and later on their same-sex friends and media characters, especially celebrities.
- Children are likely to copy gestures, body language and intonations in speech.
- As they get older and their sense of gender develops, boys are more likely to imitate their fathers and other male role models, whilst girls will be more inclined to imitate their mothers and other female models.
- The theory accounts for the considerable differences between cultures in the degree to which people stand close, touch, hug and kiss.

The role of reinforcement and punishment

People tend to imitate behaviour that is reinforced (rewarded) but avoid imitating behaviour that is punished. If behaviour such as kissing, sitting close or putting a hand on someone's shoulder receives a positive response, such as a smile or moving closer, then it is likely to be repeated. If it receives a negative response such as backing away or tension in the body, the behaviour is less likely to occur again.

Cultural variations in NVC

Personal space is like an invisible bubble surrounding us into which people cannot move without causing us discomfort. It is a form of NVC because when we move away or towards someone (quite subconsciously) we are sending a message such as "that's quite close enough thank you" or "I like you, I want to be friends with you".

Personal space is very much affected by culture. Different cultures have very different norms for how close they stand to others and how much they touch each other. Little (1968) examined cultural differences over 19 different social situations in a sample of Americans, Swedes, Greeks, Italians and Scots. They had to place dolls at distances that reflected where they would stand in real social situations, such as two good friends talking or a shop owner discussing the weather with his assistant. The findings showed considerable differences between cultures, as follows:

- The Greeks stood closest, the Americans next closest and the Scots the furthest away.
- There were considerable male–female differences between Greeks and Scots: with the Greeks it was the women who stood closer than the men but with the Scots the women stood further away than the men.
- On average across all nations there was only a small gender difference, with the men standing slightly closer than the women.

Different cultures have different norms for personal space

Contact and non-contact cultures

Hall (1966) distinguished between "contact" and "non-contact" cultures.

Contact cultures (e.g. Mediterranean countries such as Italy and Spain, Latin American countries and many countries in the Middle East)	Non-contact cultures (e.g. Britain, other northern European countries and the USA)
Lots of physical contact between people	Limited physical contact
People enjoy the company of others	People keep themselves to themselves
Lots of social mixing	Not a great deal of informal socialising
View people from non-contact cultures as standoffish and snobbish, and feel offended by the distance they keep	View people from contact countries as invasive, intrusive, overfamiliar and are embarrassed and uncomfortable with them

Contact and non-contact cultures have different notions of what is appropriate behaviour in terms of personal space, so their notions of what is reinforcing and what is punishing are also very different. People from non-contact countries feel that people from contact countries are overbearing and intrusive. People from contact countries believe that those from non-contact countries are standoffish and snobby. Their different experiences of appropriate behaviour in terms of NVC can therefore lead to misunderstanding. This emphasises the important role that reinforcement and punishment have in NVC.

Criticisms of social learning theory of NVC

- *It cannot account for NVC that is universal*: Social learning theory is useful in being able to account for cultural (and subcultural) differences in NVC. It follows that if behaviour is different between cultures then it must be learnt, not innate. However, there are many aspects of NVC that are *universal* (i.e. the same across the world), such as the facial expression for certain emotions: happiness and sadness, for example, are recognised in all cultures.
- *It underestimates the extent to which NVC is innate*: Following on from the last point, social learning theory underestimates the extent to which certain NVC is "hard wired" into us.
- *It overemphasises the role of learning in NVC*: Again, it follows that social learning theory exaggerates the extent to which NVC is the result of observation and imitation.

Evolutionary theory and NVC

An alternative approach to social learning as an explanation for NVC comes from evolutionary theory. The following provide support for this:

- *Similarities between humans and monkeys in NVC*: For example, certain facial expressions, especially in showing emotion; the use of touch in order to greet; the use of the same gestures, such as pointing and beckoning; certain postures for dominance and submission.
- *Some human signals (e.g. smiling) are innate rather than learnt*: Smiling appears in all cultures (however isolated), and in blind children who obviously cannot observe it.

Using both theories to explain NVC

Neither social learning theory nor evolutionary theory can entirely explain NVC. Social learning theory can account for cultural and subcultural differences in NVC, whereas evolutionary theory can account for universal patterns of NVC both across species and across cultures. Probably, many aspects of NVC (such as facial expression to show basic emotions, and gestures such as pointing) have evolved and then been modified by social learning.

CORE STUDY: YUKI ET AL. (2007)

Aim: To see if there was any difference in the way in which Japanese and American people judge whether a face is happy or sad.

Method: Groups of Japanese and American students were asked to rate how happy or sad various computer-generated emoticons seemed to them. The researchers then did the same using photographs of real faces, which they manipulated in order to control the degree to which the eyes and mouth were happy, sad or neutral.

An emoticon is a symbol or combination of symbols used to convey emotional content in written or message form

Results:
- *The Japanese gave more weight to eyes* of the emoticons and the real faces when gauging emotions.
- *The Americans gave more weight to the mouth* of both emoticons and real faces when judging emotions.

Conclusion: The way we express emotion varies from culture to culture and therefore must, to a certain extent, be learned rather than innate.

Limitations:

1. *Lack of ecological validity*. There are at least two ways in which the study lacks ecological validity:
   - The emoticons are a very simplified version of a real face so the study does not necessarily tell us about other features that might be important in judging emotion in a face.
   - The participants were not given cues from movements of the face or body language, both of which may be used to judge emotion in real life.
2. *Biased sample of participants*. Only students were used in this study, so they may not be representative of the target population.

How psychological research relates to social skills training

Social skills training as a treatment for offenders

Many offenders lack basic social skills such as controlling their anger or making appropriate eye contact. Social skills training is aimed at improving the ability to cope with ordinary social interactions. A programme may teach the following:

1. *Micro-skills* – certain basic non-verbal skills such as eye contact, gesture and posture.
2. *All-round skills* – for example, how to maintain a good conversation, how to interact with members of the opposite sex or how to negotiate.

There are a variety of such programmes, all of which use the following techniques to teach people these basic skills:

- *Modelling* – where an actor (or more than one actor) shows people how to behave in certain situations.
- *Instruction* – being coached on what to do.
- *Role play* – being placed in a certain situation (e.g. imagining you are being interviewed for a job or that you are going on a first date) and advised about how to play the part.
- *Rehearsal* – repeating the skills until they have been achieved to a reasonable standard.

EVALUATION

➕ Spence et al. (1981) reported that several programmes improved the self-esteem of those taking part and gave them a feeling of greater control over their lives.

➖ Other studies indicate that only about 10–15% of trainees could use these skills in real-life situations outside the training programmes.

⊕ Nevertheless, 50% could do so once given additional help.

⊕ Social skills training programmes appear to help people acquire these skills in the short term but whether this helps them in the long term in the "real" world is less certain.

OVER TO YOU

Now try the following revision activities:

1. Draw a table of two columns, one headed "Contact cultures" and the other headed "Non-contact cultures". Fill in the table by giving three characteristics of each type of culture arranged, so they are describing differences between them (e.g. lots of social mixing/very little informal socialising).
2. Test yourself on the Yuki et al. (2007) study by writing the headings "Aim", "Method", "Results", "Conclusion" and filling in the details. Go back and compare it with your textbook.
3. Write the following words/phrases on one side of separate pieces of card and the definition on the other:
    - Posture
    - Open posture
    - Closed posture
    - Postural echo
    Then use the cards to test yourself on the meaning of these terms.

EXAMPLE EXAM QUESTIONS

1 Outline **two** examples of cultural differences in non-verbal communication. **4 MARKS**

2 Describe one way in which the study of non-verbal communication has been applied to social skills training. **4 MARKS**

3 Describe and evaluate how social learning theory explains non-verbal communication. **6 MARKS**

MODEL ANSWER TO QUESTION 3

Note that on a question carrying this number of marks you will be judged on Quality of Written Communication, *so in order to gain top marks you need to write in full sentences with good spelling and punctuation, and use appropriate psychological terminology.*

According to social learning theory, people learn by observing other people and imitating them. The people who are copied are called models. The main models for young children are their parents, especially the same-sex parents, and they will imitate their non-verbal communication. For example, they will learn how much to touch other people, what kind of non-verbal greeting to give various people and how far away you stand when having a conversation. They are particularly likely to repeat behaviour that is reinforced, so, for example, they will repeat behaviour that receives a smile or cuddle.

One problem with social learning theory is that it cannot explain non-verbal communication that is the same across all cultures, such as smiling, frowning or showing fear. Because these behaviours are universal, they appear to be innate and not learned.

Notice that you do not need a great deal of evaluation provided that the meaning is clear and it uses appropriate terminology. In this example, the term "innate" is used in the evaluation.

11

INDIVIDUAL DIFFERENCES: The Self

What's it about?

Some psychologists are interested in why people differ from each other. This area is called "individual differences". One way to look at this is the development of the self. Every person has different experiences of the world and this must mould who they are and why they act in a particular way. If we look at this in more depth then we may also be able to help people out who have had negative experience through counselling and therapy.

WHAT'S IN THIS UNIT?

The specification lists the following things that you will need to be able to do for the examination:

- Understand the idea that individuals are unique
- Explain the concept of free will
- Distinguish between self-concept and ideal self in relation to self-esteem
- Explain the idea of unconditional positive regard
- Explain the idea of self-actualisation
- Explain the criticisms of humanism as an explanation of the self
- Consider trait theory as an alternative theory, with specific reference to extraversion and neuroticism
- Describe and outline the limitations of the van Houtte and Jarvis (1995) study
- Application of research into the self, e.g. counselling

Key terms

Here is a list of important terms that you should learn in your revision. Try to write definitions for these after reading the chapter, and check your answers in the glossary on pp. 129–135. Essential terms that you *must* know in order to properly understand the topic are marked with an asterisk.

Congruence	Person-centred therapy	Trait theory
Empathy	Self-actualisation*	Unconditional positive
Free will*	Self-concept*	regard*
Ideal self*	Self-esteem*	

Individuals are unique

The humanist movement in psychology has the idea that individuals are unique, moulded by the experiences that they have. As we all have different experiences, we are all unique. Everyone has their own potential to fulfil their capabilities, and this needs nurturing by ourselves and by others. As a result, no two individuals are the same.

Free will

One of the key ideas of humanism is that we all have **free will**. This term refers to us all making conscious choices about the way we live.

Self-concept, ideal self and self-esteem

- **Self-concept** refers to the mental image that we have of ourselves, which features physical and psychological attributes. This can be made up of our current self (how we are now) but we could add elements from our ideal self.
- **Ideal self** refers to our mental representation of who we ideally would like to be.
- **Self-esteem** refers to how we *feel* about our current self. If we do not like much about our self-concept then we will have low self-esteem. If we quite like our self-concept and can see positive aspects then we will have high self-esteem.

Unconditional positive regard

Unconditional positive regard occurs when a person is completely accepting of another no matter what. You are completely accepting of that person in terms of things you like, and ignore the bad side. It is unconditional because you expect nothing in return.

Self-actualisation

Self-actualisation refers to us reaching and fulfilling our own potential. Maslow stated that self-actualisation is at the pinnacle of our hierarchy of needs and that we need to progress with other things in our lives first. Below is a diagram showing our hierarchy of needs according to Maslow.

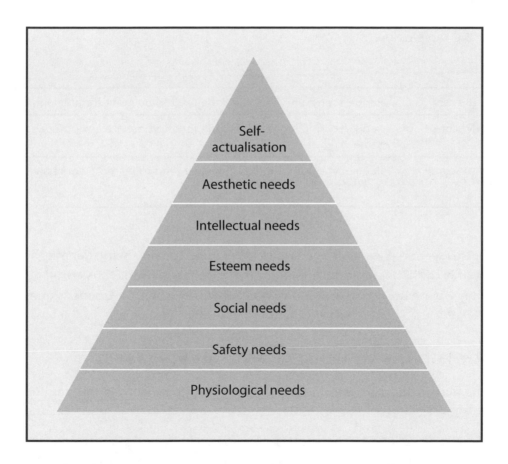

Self-actualisation

Aesthetic needs

Intellectual needs

Esteem needs

Social needs

Safety needs

Physiological needs

Criticisms of humanism

- There are other plausible explanations for personality. For example, Eysenck believed that we all have differing levels of things such as extraversion and introversion, and that personality can be categorised.

- The theory is culture-bound, as other cultures place much more emphasis on group work in fulfilling themselves rather than on the North American ideal of individualism.
- The concept of free will can be questioned by its opposite: determinism. There is evidence to suggest that some aspects of self are determined at birth (temperament).
- The ideas of self-actualisation, unconditional positive regard and free will are very subjective and based on opinions.

Trait theory: Eysenck's approach to personality

Eysenck's approach attempts to identify different personality types. Eysenck created the Eysenck Personality Questionnaire (EPQ) to measure the personality types of people using some yes/no questions. Once completed, a score can be given to show the level of his personality factors, which are shown in the table below.

Extraversion (E score)	People scoring high on this scale tend to be more sociable and impulsive
Neuroticism (N score)	People scoring high on this scale tend to be more anxious, depressed and tense
Psychoticism (P score)	People who score high on this scale tend to be more aggressive, egocentric and cold

Finally for this section, Eysenck was a firm believer in personality being genetic (he claimed up to two-thirds of it could be), therefore some of these traits are fixed. Thus we all have a core of personality that we are born with and this affects our E–P–N scores on Eysenck's questionnaire.

CORE STUDY: VAN HOUTTE AND JARVIS (1995)

Aim: The aim of this study was to examine the role of pets in pre-adolescent (8–12 years of age) psychosocial development.

Procedure: A sample of 130 pre-adolescents aged 8–12 years of age completed a range of questionnaires. These included measures of *autonomy*, *self-concept* and *self-esteem* (how you feel about yourself). Additionally, all participants completed a measure on their attachment to animals. There were two groups of participants: a pet-owning group and a non-pet-owning group. However, for each pet-owning participant, a non-pet-owning participant was *matched* for parental marital status, socioeconomic status and number of siblings. Therefore it was a *matched pairs design*.

Results:

- *Autonomy*: Higher levels of autonomy were reported in pet owners across all participants irrespective of age.
- *Self-concept*: The only instance when the pet owners significantly differed from non-pet-owners was in sixth-graders. Their self-concept was significantly higher.
- *Self-esteem*: Those who owned a pet reported significantly higher self-esteem compared to the non-pet-owning group.
- *Attachment to animals in general*: There was no difference between the two groups of participants.

Conclusion: Pets could be used to enhance self-concept and increase self-esteem for pre-adolescents with low levels of both.

Limitations:

- There were small sample sizes in each of the age groups.
- The participants completed questionnaires, which could lead to two problems: there is no way of knowing if the participants were telling the truth; and there could have been some demand characteristics happening with the questionnaires, with the participants working out the aim of the study.
- As the work was not truly experimental there could have been other factors common to the pet-owning group that affected the measures rather than simply owning a pet.

Counselling

A humanistic counsellor would help to explore ideas that could be frustrating the client and making them unhappy. Also, there is very little focus on past happenings. This type of counselling is based on the work of Carl Rogers. The focus is on the present and future, and how things can change there, using:

1. *Empathy* – the therapist's ability to understand how the client is feeling about life experiences.
2. *Congruence*, sometimes called *genuineness*. This refers to the therapist allowing the client to experience them for who they are.
3. *Unconditional positive regard* – maintaining a positive attitude towards the client no matter what.

...warmth, acceptance and empathy on the part of the therapist.

Therefore, a client is treated as being unique. They are nurtured to help them grow to their own full potential, with the main goal being to self-actualise, which should then increase self-esteem and self-worth.

OVER TO YOU

Now try the following revision activities:

1. Type up the van Houtte and Jarvis study into short sentences that cover the aim, all of the procedure, all of the results and then the conclusion. Cut out each sentence and muddle them all up. Then, place them back in the correct order.
2. There are many definitions to learn for this topic. Get some index cards and write the term on one side of the card and its definition on the other. Then, get someone to test you on your definitions.
3. To help you understand Eysenck's theory of personality, create three questions you would ask people to see if they scored high on neuroticism. Then repeat this for extraversion and introversion.

EXAMPLE EXAM QUESTIONS

1 Define the term *unconditional positive regard*.   **2 MARKS**

2 Outline **two** criticisms of humanism.   **4 MARKS**

3 Describe the procedure of the van Houtte and Jarvis (1995) study.   **4 MARKS**

4 Distinguish between self-concept and the ideal self in relation to self-esteem.   **3 MARKS**

MODEL ANSWER TO QUESTION 2

The first criticism of humanism is that it could be culturally specific. Not all cultures favour being an individual and Eastern cultures are sometime called collectivist as they prefer to work in groups. Humanism finds it hard to explain this. A second criticism is that some bits of personality may be genetic (e.g. temperament), which is in contrast to the free will argument that we always make our own decisions.

RESEARCH IN PSYCHOLOGY

12

What's it about?

This chapter covers all the research methods in psychology and the issues that arise from them. A lot of this you will have covered as you revised the other chapters, so hopefully this will not be unfamiliar to you. The Unit 3 exam is devoted to research methods but additional questions on this topic will appear throughout all the exam papers, so be prepared for that.

WHAT'S IN THIS UNIT?

The specification lists the following things that you will need to be able to do for the examination:

Planning research

- Hypotheses
- Variables
- Experimental design
- Sampling techniques
- Ethical considerations

Analysing research

- Types of data
- Descriptive data
- Tables, charts and graphs
- Evaluating findings
- Sources of bias

Doing research

- Experiments
- Questionnaires
- Interviews
- Observations
- Types of studies

Planning an investigation

- Investigation skills
- Design skills

Planning research

Hypotheses

When a psychological investigation is done, the researcher starts with an aim and a hypothesis.

The *aim* of a study is usually one sentence that clearly highlights what the researcher is intending to investigate. The *hypothesis* is a prediction. It is a sentence that states what the researcher predicts the findings could be.

The investigator starts with two different hypotheses:

- An *alternative hypothesis* states that there will be a difference between two sets of scores, or a correlation between them (depending on the type of study that was done). It is a clear specific statement such as: "Children who have watched an aggressive model will show a greater number of aggressive acts than children who have watched a non-aggressive model."
- A *null hypothesis* states that there will be no difference or relationship between two sets of scores. An example is: "There will be no difference in the amount of aggression shown between children who have watched an aggressive model and children who have watched a non-aggressive model."

You will notice that the alternative and the null hypothesis cannot both be true. The purpose of an investigation is to decide which one is more likely to be true and therefore to choose between them.

Variables

One of the research methods used by psychologists is an experiment. An experiment involves the deliberate manipulation of one variable to measure its effect on another variable while keeping all other variables constant (as far as possible). The **independent variable (IV)** is the variable the psychologist deliberately manipulates, whereas the **dependent variable (DV)** is the variable that is measured to see if it has been affected by the IV (see Activity on p. 306 of *Psychology for GCSE Level, 2nd Edition*, to make sure you understand these variables).

Extraneous (confounding) variables are any variables that might affect the findings and give us false results. The main ways in which these are controlled are as follows:

- Keep all aspects of the situation the same. This controls for **situational variables**.
- If we are using two groups of participants, make sure they are as similar as possible. This controls for **participant variables**.
- Follow the same procedure for every participant. These procedures are called **standardised procedures**.
- Give the same instructions to every participant in a particular condition. These are called **standardised instructions**.

Experimental design (participant design)

Design	Description	Advantages	Disadvantages	Points to note
Independent groups design	Two or more separate groups of participants are used, one group in each condition of the IV	Can be used in cases where a repeated measures design cannot be used because the investigation requires separate groups, such as a comparison of men and women, young people and old people, urban and rural dwellers	There may be important differences between the groups of individuals to start with and these, rather than the IV, may be responsible for differences in results	Important to match the groups as a whole on important characteristics, especially those that might affect the DV. Alternatively, use random allocation of participants to each condition
Repeated measures design	The same participants are used in all conditions of the study	Controls for individual differences between participants (participant variables)	Introduces problems of **order effects**, i.e. **practice effects** and **fatigue/boredom**	Usually needs **counterbalancing** to offset the problem of order effects

independent groups   *Repeated measures*

Sampling techniques

The **target population** is the whole population in which a researcher is interested. The aim of a researcher is to select a **sample** from this target population and to try to get a **representative sample**. Any sample that is not representative is a *biased sample*. The following sampling methods are ones you should know.

Random sampling

- A **random sample** is a sample in which every member of the target population has an equal chance of being selected. This is likely to give you a representative sample but is difficult to use in practice.
- An **opportunity sample** is one that uses anyone who is available and willing to take part. It is an easy and practical sample to use but is biased rather than representative.
- A **volunteer (self-selected) sample** consists of people who have offered to take part in a study, perhaps by answering an advertisement. It is unlikely to provide a representative sample because there is no reason to believe that volunteers are typical of everyone in the target population.

Ethical considerations

Ethical guidelines are extremely important when planning research.

Ethical issues	Ways of dealing with them
Deception: Participants should not be deceived unless it is absolutely necessary	Deception should be minimal and a full debrief explaining the need for deception should be offered
Informed consent: Wherever possible the informed consent of the participant should be obtained	If this is impractical, a full debrief should be given
Confidentiality: Any personal information obtained in a study should be completely confidential	Participants must give permission beforehand if the researcher wants the results to be shared or published
Debriefing: Participants should, where possible, be debriefed	The participant should be informed of the true nature and purpose of the study at the end
Withdrawal from the investigation: It should be made clear to participants that they are free to withdraw from the investigation at any time	If participants look upset, the researcher should offer them the chance to withdraw
Protection of participants: Participants should not be placed under any great stress, nor should they be harmed, either physically or mentally	Stop a study if it looks as if the participants are under stress

Doing research

Experiments

An **experiment** involves the deliberate manipulation of an independent variable to measure its effect on a dependent variable while keeping all other variables constant (as far as possible).

Types of experiments

Type of experiment	Description	Positive points	Negative points (limitations/problems)
Laboratory experiment	Experiments carried out in very tightly controlled surroundings, often with special equipment available	These are the only experiments that allow confident conclusions about cause and effect, due to the fact that the confounding variables can be controlled	The study may therefore lack **ecological validity** because it does not reflect ordinary behaviour. The results of the study do not necessarily tell us much about everyday behaviour
Field experiment	Experiments carried out in everyday surroundings but still with manipulation of the IV	Behaviour in a field experiment is far more natural than in a laboratory setting, so this has greater ecological validity – it tells us more about ordinary everyday behaviour	It is not possible to have such tight control over variables in the field, so we cannot be so confident of cause and effect; other factors could influence the DV

Questionnaires

A **questionnaire** is a list of questions given to participants. Questionnaires are used in surveys and are particularly useful when trying to investigate people's attitudes. They are a form of *self-report*.

A questionnaire may contain one of two types of questions:

1. *Closed questions*: These have fixed alternative responses, such as: strongly agree, agree, uncertain, disagree, strongly disagree; yes/no.

EVALUATION

➕ Closed questions are quick to answer and score, and provide information that is useful in making comparisons – e.g. that 54% of people remember their first day at school.

➖ They provide a very limited amount of information and leave no room for responses such as "it depends on . . .". They therefore lack validity (are not an accurate reflection of people's opinions).

2. *Open questions*: These give respondents the chance to express themselves more freely. For example: "Describe everything you can remember about your first day at school."

EVALUATION

➕ Open questions provide a source of rich and detailed information.

➖ They take a lot longer to score and, since all responses are different, it is much more difficult to make comparisons between individuals or summarise data across groups.

EVALUATION OF QUESTIONNAIRES

➕ They allow researchers to study large samples of people fairly easily.

➕ With closed questions, it is possible to generalise the results to a larger population.

➕ Questionnaires with open questions are a way of obtaining information about attitudes that would be difficult to obtain in any other way.

➖ People may not respond truthfully, either because they cannot remember or because they wish to present themselves in a socially acceptable manner.

➖ It may be difficult to get a representative sample of participants to complete the questionnaire.

Interviews

A **structured interview** involves a list of questions that require the interviewee to choose from a selection of possible answers. It is basically a verbal means of presenting a questionnaire that has closed questions. Like a questionnaire, it is a method of *self-report*.

EVALUATION

➕ It is easy to make comparisons between people because they all answer exactly the same questions.

➖ You can only gain a limited amount of information, none of which is in-depth.

An **unstructured interview** is a more lengthy interview aimed at a detailed understanding of a person's mental processes. There are no set questions; the questions depend on the last answer given.

EVALUATION

➕ Unstructured interviews provide rich insight into the thoughts of individual children or adults, which a standardised format would not allow.

➖ It is impossible to interview everyone in the same way, so it is almost impossible to compare responses of different people.

Observations

An **observation** involves watching people (or animals) and recording and analysing their behaviour.

Covert and overt observations

- **Covert observations** are those in which the observer remains hidden or at least blends in with the scenery so does not affect the behaviour of those being observed.
- **Overt observations** are those in which the observers make themselves known to the people being observed.

Participant and non-participant observation

- In **participant observation** the observers take an active part in the group or situation by becoming members of the group they are studying.
- **Non-participant observation** is any observation in which the observer remains separate from the people being observed.

Advantages and disadvantages of different types of observations		
Type of observation	Positive points	Negative points
Covert	This is usually a **naturalistic observation**; it has high ecological validity and tells us something valid about real-life behaviour	It's difficult for observers to remain hidden and still record their observations accurately
Overt	By making themselves known, they can observe quite closely and keep careful records of their observations	Once observers make themselves known to the people they are observing, they affect their behaviour, so the observations have low ecological validity – they do not reflect real-life behaviour
Participant	By becoming part of a group, the observer can gain much greater insight into the behaviour of the participants than if they remain an outsider	There are ethical problems involved in joining a group and observing them. It is important to respect confidentiality and privacy
Non-participant	If this is a naturalistic observation in which the observer remains hidden, it has high ecological validity and tells us something valid about real-life behaviour	It can be difficult for observers to be inconspicuous and still record their observations accurately

Carrying out observations

In order to carry out a good observational study the following things are necessary:

- For all observers involved in the same research operation to have a clear idea of exactly what they are observing.
- To use a system for categorising and recording behaviour.
- To use either a recording device (such as a video camera) or more than one observer.

Categories of behaviour in observations

The researcher has to decide on the categories of behaviour they are interested in. For example, for "aggression" it could be punching, kicking, hitting, verbal abuse and so on. For attachment it could be smiling at carer, moving towards carer, being upset when carer moves away, clinging to carer, looking at carer and so on.

Inter-observer reliability

It is important that observers looking at the same behaviour should categorise it in the same way. Inter-observer reliability is the extent to which there is agreement between observers. Inter-observer reliability is high if there is a considerable amount of agreement, but low if there is little agreement. Obviously a study that has low inter-observer reliability is a poor one.

Types of studies

Case studies

A **case study** is a detailed investigation of a single individual or a small group of individuals.

A positive correlation: The taller the player, the higher the score.

EVALUATION

➕ Case studies are useful for investigating the effects of unusual experiences such as deprivation, hospitalisation or unusual educational experiences.

➖ Case studies only relate to one individual or small group and we cannot therefore generalise to others from the result.

➖ There is a danger that the psychologist who looks at a case study may get very involved and not be entirely unbiased.

A negative correlation: The more time spent playing computer games, the less time spent studying.

Correlations

A correlational study involves taking lots of *pairs* of scores and seeing if there is a positive or negative relationship (a **correlation**) between them.

The direction of a correlation

- A **positive correlation** means that high values of one variable are associated with high values of the other.
- A **negative correlation** means that high values of one variable are associated with low values of the other.
- If there is *no* correlation between two variables they are said to be **uncorrelated**.

No correlation: Where there is no relationship, variables are uncorrelated.

The strength of a correlation

Some correlations are strong, others are weak. For example, students who spend many hours a week reading novels tend to score highly on vocabulary tests; this is a strong positive correlation.

Students who spend many hours a week reading novels tend to perform slightly better than average on science tests; this is a weak positive correlation.

Correlations can be represented in the form of a graph called a *scattergraph* (or scattergram), with a dot for each participant indicating where he or she falls on the two dimensions.

EVALUATION

➕ Correlations are very useful for making predictions. If two variables are correlated, you can predict one from the other.

➖ Correlations only show that a relationship exists between two variables. They do NOT show that one *causes* the other. There could be a third factor that is causing both. See pp. 321–322 of *Psychology for GCSE Level, 2nd Edition*.

Designing studies

Longitudinal studies follow the *same* participants over a long period of time.

EVALUATION

➕ Longitudinal studies allow researchers to see the long-term effects of upbringing and experiences.

➖ Some participants may drop out and this can leave a biased sample because those who drop out are not necessarily typical of the rest of the group.

Cross-sectional studies also look at changes over time, but by comparing people of different ages.

EVALUATION

➕ Cross-sectional studies are much quicker and easier than longitudinal studies.

➖ Differences between the groups may not be due to age but to other factors such as educational background or differences in cultural norms. This is known as the cohort effect. See p. 313 of *Psychology for GCSE Level, 2nd Edition*.

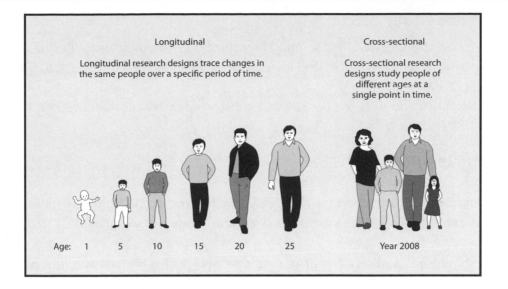

Analysing research

Types of data

- *Quantitative data*: This term refers to data that take the form of numbers.
- *Qualitative data*: This term refers to data that take the form of words (or any data that are not in the form of numbers).

Quantitative data are very useful if we want to make comparisons between groups (e.g. the mean amount remembered by two groups working under different conditions). Qualitative data are useful if we want in-depth detailed information, such as in a case study or concerning people's attitudes.

Descriptive data

Measures of central tendency		
Type of measure	What it is	How to use it
The mean	This is the sum of all the scores divided by the number of scores	This takes account of all scores and is useful as long as there are no very unusual scores
The median	This is the middle number in a data set after you have placed them in rank order	This is useful with a set of scores in which there are any unusual (extreme) ones
The mode	This is the most frequent score	Useful if you want to know the most popular opinion or the most frequent behaviour of people

Measure of dispersion

It is useful to know the spread of the scores. The easiest way to do this is to use the *range*, which is the difference between the highest and lowest scores. So, in the set of scores 4, 5, 5, 7, 7, 8, 9, 12, the range is 8 (12 – 4).

The range is quick and easy to calculate but is distorted by an anomalous score.

Tables, charts and graphs

- *Tables* should be used to *summarise* data, so that whoever is reading it can make sense of the numbers. A table may show the mean, median and mode of two groups of scores alongside the range.
- *Bar charts* should be used to *summarise* data that are already in separate groups (e.g. males/females).
- *Line graphs* are used when you are plotting data that are *continuous* along the bottom axis and you want to show a trend.

Evaluating findings

To evaluate a study you can write about validity and reliability.

Validity

Validity means how "real" the findings are. One type of validity is *ecological validity*. This term refers to how much the findings reflect the real-life or real-world behaviour of the participants. This can include where the study was set and the task given to participants.

Reliability

Reliability means consistency, so you can evaluate how easy it is to replicate (repeat) a study to see if you *could* get similar results.

- With respect to an observation study, it is important to know how reliable your observers were (called *inter-observer reliability*).
- If the study is in a laboratory then you could argue that it is reliable because the high level of controls makes it *easier* to replicate.

Other issues

- *Demand characteristics*: This term refers to the situation in which a participant works out what the aim of the study is and then acts according to that rather than to their true beliefs.

- *Observer effect*: This is a situation in which people change their behaviour because they know they are being observed. This can reduce the validity of the findings.
- *Social desirability*: This occurs when a participant wants to *look good* to the researchers. This reduces the validity of the findings as the participant is not reporting their true opinions.

Sources of bias

Gender bias

This type of bias can come about in two different ways:

- There is a gender imbalance in the sample of participants that could affect the results.
- The sex of the researcher. Participants may react differently if there is a male researcher compared to a female researcher.

Cultural bias

This type of bias can come about if the task or study gives an unfair advantage to one culture over another.

Experimenter bias

This type of bias can come about in a variety of ways:

- The experimenter may give away too much information in the brief or standardised instructions, causing demand characteristics in the participants.
- The experimenter's belief about what they are studying can affect the results of that study.
- How the experimenter interacts with the participant (e.g. how friendly or curt they are) can affect motivation in the participant.

Planning an investigation

In the examination you may be asked to plan an investigation based on a stimulus provided in the exam (a brief outline of what you need to investigate). The method will be specified and chosen from an experiment, questionnaire, interview or observation.

Investigation skills

For any investigation, you need to be able to:

- State the hypothesis for the investigation.
- Describe and justify the sample used in an investigation.

- Describe ethical issues involved in an investigation.
- Describe and justify how the variables are measured in an investigation.
- Describe and justify the control of extraneous variables in an investigation.
- Describe the procedure used in an investigation.
- Explain the strengths of the method used in an investigation.
- Explain the weaknesses of the method used in an investigation.
- Describe how data are analysed in an investigation.

All of these points have been covered in the chapter, so here we are going to consider how to answer questions on the exam paper. See pp. 333–334 of *Psychology for GCSE Level, 2nd Edition*, for suggestions of investigations that you could be asked to plan.

Design skills

When answering such exam questions, we will take the list of items you need to know and consider some important points.

- *State the hypothesis for the investigation*: When writing an alternative hypothesis for your planned investigation, make sure you clearly identify the variables and that they have been operationalised. Do not, for example, say that "memory" will be better in one condition than another but say precisely what has been measured (e.g. number of words recalled).
- *Describe and justify the sample used in an investigation*: Make sure you can distinguish between each of the sampling methods – random, opportunity and volunteer (self-selected).
- *Describe ethical issues involved in an investigation*: Make sure you know all the ethical issues: deception, consent, confidentiality, debriefing, right to withdraw from the investigation, protection of participants, use of children as participants. When answering an exam question, always refer to the particular ethical issue you are dealing with rather than simply say what you would do about it.
- *Describe and justify how the variables are measured in an investigation*: Think carefully about how you could measure the variables. In an observation study remember that you need categories of behaviour.
- *Describe and justify the control of extraneous variables in an investigation*: This is very largely common sense. Use standardised procedure and standardised instructions. If carrying out an interview, use the same interviewer for everyone.
- *Describe the procedure used in an investigation*: The best way to approach this is to think about what you would need to do if you were carrying out the study and then go through it in a systematic way. Don't forget to include essential relevant procedures such as writing a questionnaire, how your participant sample was chosen, how your participants were divided into groups, the standardised instructions they were given, how the variables were measured and so on.

- *Explain the strengths/weaknesses of the method used in an investigation*: Make sure you know the strengths and weaknesses of each of the four methods you could be asked to use, and think about how they might be relevant.
- *Describe how data are analysed in an investigation*: Think about whether you will obtain qualitative or quantitative data (or both) and the advantages and disadvantages of each. Consider also the type of graph you may draw, the measure of central tendency (mean, median, mode) that would be best, whether it is appropriate to give the range of scores and so on.

Finally, consider how you would answer questions concerning:

- Sources of bias (gender bias, cultural bias, experimenter bias).
- Reliability, particularly inter-rater reliability. How could you try to ensure that it was high? How could you test it?
- Validity, particularly ecological validity.
- Problems of demand characteristics, observer effect and social desirability.

EXAMPLE EXAM QUESTIONS

1 A psychology student used a laboratory experiment to conduct a study of memory. She asked her friends if they would take part and used them as participants.

(a) Outline **one** problem with using a laboratory experiment to investigate memory. **2 MARKS**

(b) What is the name given to the sampling method used? **1 MARK**

(c) Outline **one** disadvantage of using this sampling method. **2 MARKS**

(d) Outline **one** ethical consideration she must bear in mind when conducting the study. **2 MARKS**

2 (a) Explain what is meant by participant observation. **2 MARKS**

(b) Outline **one** advantage of a participant observation. **2 MARKS**

(c) Explain the difference between a covert and an overt observation study. **2 MARKS**

3 Planning an investigation. You have been asked to plan an experiment to investigate whether people remember more when in the same environment they learnt it in than in a different environment. You are to carry out the research in a lesson at your school so the method used will be a field experiment.

(a) State what the dependent variable is in your investigation and say how it will be measured. **2 MARKS**

(b) State an alternative hypothesis for the investigation. **2 MARKS**

(c) Describe **one** ethical issue you would have to deal with when carrying out this study. **3 MARKS**

(d) Explain the procedure of the study. **3 MARKS**

(e) What participant design would you use in this study? **1 MARK**

(f) Give **one** weakness of the participant design you have chosen and say why this would be a weakness in this particular experiment. **2 MARKS**

(g) Describe **one** extraneous variable that was controlled in this study and why it was necessary to control it. **2 MARKS**

MODEL ANSWER TO QUESTION 3

(a) The dependent variable is the amount recalled. I would measure this by asking a teacher to devise some questions about the lesson and seeing how many questions the students got correct in each of the two conditions.

(b) People will answer more questions correctly when in the same room in which they learnt the work than in a different room.

(c) I would have to consider the issue of informed consent. I could not tell the participants the exact nature of the study but I would ask their consent to take part in a study and assure them that they would have a full explanation of the purpose of the study after it was completed.

(d) I would ask a teacher if the study could take place in their lesson and devise a set of questions that the students could answer at the end of their lesson. I would explain the purpose of the study in full to the teacher and ask him or her to gain the consent of the students by explaining to them that they would be taking part in a simple exercise to look at the best conditions to learn in and that they would be told the details at the end of the study, but that it would not involve them doing anything very different from what might take place in an ordinary lesson. I would ask the teacher to confidentially split the class into two so that each half was of roughly the same ability. The lesson would then take place as normal, but 10 minutes from the end all the students would be asked to leave the room very briefly. One half would be asked to return to the same room, while the other half would be asked to go a different room. I would give the test questions to one group to answer in silence, whilst my friend would give the questions to the other group, also in silence. We would then ask the teacher to mark the work and give us the results for each group.

(e) I would use an independent groups design.

(f) One weakness of an independent groups design is individual differences between the participants. In this case, it is possible that the students in one condition have a better memory (or pay more attention) than the students in the other group.

(g) I sent both groups out of the room at the end of the first part of the study rather than just sending one group into another room so that one group did not have an unfair advantage over the other. It is possible that having to move could affect the ability to remember.

GLOSSARY

Accessibility: the readiness with which information that has already been processed can be located.

Active/discovery learning: when a child learns through his or her own actions and is not explicitly taught, e.g. children in preschool learn about the properties of water through "water-play".

Androgyny: a set of behaviours that include high levels of both masculine and feminine characteristics.

Anonymous: having no known name, source or identifying features. Used to maintain participants' confidentiality in psychological research.

Association: forming a learned connection between a stimulus and a response, or between one stimulus and another.

Attachment bond: a long-enduring, emotionally meaningful tie to a particular individual.

Authoritarian personality: according to Adorno, a person with this type of personality is intolerant of others with differing views, is dominating, is attracted to groups where there are strong leaders and respects higher authority figures.

Authority figure: someone who is regarded by others as having power over a situation or group, e.g. researchers in Milgram's obedience studies.

Availability: whether or not information that may already have been processed in the brain is still available to be accessed.

Aversion therapy: a method of decreasing unwanted behaviours using the principle of associating a noxious stimulus with an already conditioned stimulus to produce a desired conditioned response.

Behaviour modification: involves using the theories of learning to change behaviour.

Body language: a type of non-verbal communication involving posture, gestures and touch. It is the way we stand and walk, and the gestures we use to convey information.

Boredom: tedious tasks within research may make participants less likely to perform in ways that reflect accurate abilities.

Bottom-up processing: when information arrives from our senses, it sets a pattern recognition process into motion. The combination of these simple data allows us then to perceive more complex patterns. Therefore, perception is solely influenced by our sensory input.

Brain damage: in relation to memory, this refers to the physical deterioration of brain structures involved in memory storage.

Brain dysfunction: a condition in which the brain does not function as it should.

Case study: detailed investigation of a single individual or a small group of individuals.

Castration anxiety: the Freudian concept that, during the phallic stage, boys fear castration by their father.

Chromosomes: strands of DNA that carry genetic information.

Classical conditioning: when an organism "learns" through establishing associations between different events and stimuli.

Clinical interview: an unstructured interview through which a researcher hopes to gain insight into an individual's thought processes.

Collectivist: cultures that tend to emphasise teamwork or working as a complete family unit and place less emphasis on individuality and independence.

Colour constancy: when we can still perceive the correct colour of an object under different light levels.

Concrete operational stage: the third developmental stage, characterised by children learning to think logically about concrete events (e.g. maths equations, science experiments).

Conditioned stimulus: the name given to the neutral stimulus after the association with the unconditioned stimulus has been conditioned.

Confederates: people who pretend to be participants in psychological research, but are in fact aware of the research aim and have been told how to respond by the researchers.

Conformity: adjusting one's behaviour or thinking to match those of other people or a group "standard".

Congruence: sometimes called *genuineness*. This refers to the therapist allowing the client to experience them for who they are.

Consensus view: agreement between the people of a society. Basically, if this system is used, actions are considered to be crimes if most people within the group agree that they should be.

Conservation: the ability to understand that changing the form of a substance or object does not change its amount, overall volume or mass.

Constructivist theory of perception: a theory stating that we develop our perceptual systems over time, based on our experience and expectations.

Control group: a participant group that does not experience the IV being tested (e.g. the group that experiences silence).

Controlled (structured) observation: an observational research method carried out in conditions over which the researcher has some control, such as a laboratory or a specially designed room.

Convergence: a depth cue, based on the inward focus of the eyes with a close object.

Correlation: a statistical indicator representing the strength of a relationship between two variables. Correlations do not show cause and effect, only that a relationship exists.

Counterbalance: used with the repeated measures design to overcome the problems of practice and order effects. Involves ensuring that each condition is equally likely to be used first and second by participants.

Covert observations: observations in which the observer remains hidden or at least blends in with the scenery so does not affect the behaviour of those being observed.

Crime: any action that breaks the law of a given society.

Critical period: a biologically determined period of time during which infants are especially ready to form an attachment. Bowlby believed that if the attachment is not formed during that time, it is unlikely to be formed at all.

Cross-sectional studies: using groups of people of different age groups to examine changes over time.

Cue dependency: in order for memories to be retrieved efficiently, there must be specific similarities to the time when the information was encoded into memory. There are two types of cue dependency: "state" and "context".

Debriefing: after a participant has taken part in a study, the true aim is revealed to them. They are then thanked and asked if they have any questions.

Decay: fading of stored information in long-term memory (LTM). Although LTM is unlimited in capacity and duration, memories will fade if unused.

Decentre: the ability to step outside one's own viewpoint and see things from another's point of view.

Defiance: a desire to resist the demands of authority and *not* do as one is told.

Denial (or diffusion) of responsibility: the feeling that one is less answerable for one's behaviour because there are other people around. Any "responsibility" is shared so that no individual feels responsible.

Dependent variable (DV): an aspect of the participant's behaviour that is measured in the study.

Deprivation: a situation in which a child experiences the loss or breaking of an already formed attachment relationship.

Depth cues: a variety of cues in the environment that help us to understand depth. These are linear perspective, texture gradient, superimposition, height in plane and relative size.

Displacement: loss of information from short-term memory based on the "first in, first out" concept.

Ecological validity: the degree to which the behaviours observed and recorded in a study reflect behaviours that actually occur in natural settings.

Egocentrism: the inability to see things from anyone else's point of view.

Electra complex: an ambiguous concept that aims to adapt the Oedipus complex for female children. According to this theory, penis envy leads girls to resent their mother, and resolution only occurs when girls identify with their mother. Freud did not use this term.

Empathy: the therapist's ability to understand how the client is feeling about life experiences. They must clearly communicate this to the client.

Encoding (input): the processing of information in such a way that it can be represented internally for memory storage.

Ethical guidelines: a standardised set of rules for researchers in psychology. Key ethical considerations include informed consent, right to withdraw, confidentiality (anonymity), debriefing and protection of participants.

Evolutionary theory: a theory that attempts to account for behaviour in terms of why it is (or was) sufficiently useful to have been selected by evolutionary processes.

Experiment: the deliberate manipulation of one variable to measure its effect on another variable, while trying to keep all other variables constant. This is the only method that allows us to draw conclusions about cause and effect.

Experimental group: the participant group that experiences the IV being tested (e.g. the group subjected to loud music).

Extraneous variables: any factor or variable, other than the variable being studied, that might affect the results, therefore giving false information.

Eye contact: a form of non-verbal communication that provides feedback to others on our mood and personality, regulates the flow of conversation and expresses emotion to others.

Facial expression: one of the most important forms of non-verbal communication because it conveys emotion. The six most recognised facial expressions are surprise, fear, anger, disgust, happiness and sadness.

Family studies: a research method used to examine genetic influences of a psychological or social phenomenon (e.g. criminality). Using this method it is possible to investigate whether criminal individuals produce more criminal children than in the non-criminal population.

Fatigue: long tasks within research are tiring, which may make the task more difficult over time and therefore affect the results.

Femininity: the behaviours and ideas that are considered to be a characteristic of being female. It is also an example of sex typing.

Field experiment: an experiment where participants are (unknowingly in some cases) observed in natural settings. The researchers can still manipulate variables and observe how people react to these manipulations.

Flooding: a method of treating phobias whereby the patient is exposed to direct contact with the feared stimulus. As the body cannot sustain high levels of arousal for long, fear quickly subsides and the stimulus–fear association is broken.

Formal operational stage: the final developmental stage, characterised by children learning to think logically about abstract (unseen) events.

Free will: the conscious choices we make about the way we live and the pathways we wish to take.

Gender identity: the psychological status of being a male or a female, including an awareness of which gender you consider yourself to be.

Genetics: the idea that our genetic make-up (DNA) can explain particular phenomena, such as phobias.

Height in plane: the closer an object is to the horizon, the further away it is compared to other objects viewed in the same picture or scene.

Heritability: the extent to which characteristics are inherited.

Hierarchies: a method of outlining information in a structured way, beginning with general information and ending with specific information.

Hormones: chemicals that are secreted into the bloodstream. A hormone is released from a gland and affects a target organ.

Ideal self: our mental representation of who we ideally would like to be.

Imagery: a memory technique that encodes information as pictures (e.g. illustrations of memory models).

Independent groups design: research that uses two (or more) groups in order to make comparisons. Each group experiences only one level of the independent variable; the dependent variable remains constant.

Independent variable (IV): some aspect of the research situation that is manipulated by the researcher in order to observe whether a change occurs in another variable.

Individualistic: cultures that tend to promote independence, including being self-reliant and "thinking for yourself".

Informed consent: always applies to research participants, and refers to written or verbal consent to take part after they are given information about what they will be asked to do.

Insecure-ambivalent attachment: an insecure attachment style characterised by behaviours such as clinging to the primary caregiver and extreme distress on separation from the primary caregiver.

Insecure-avoidant attachment: an insecure attachment style characterised by behaviours that avoid contact with the primary caregiver.

Inter-observer reliability: how much two or more independent observers agree on the ratings given by the researcher prior to analysis of results. It is high if there is considerable agreement, and low if there is little agreement.

Introjection: the Freudian concept of adopting the attributes, attitudes or qualities of a highly significant person into one's own persona.

Laboratory experiment: an experiment carried out in very tightly controlled surroundings (but not necessarily a laboratory), often with special equipment.

Levels of processing: a theory stating that memories are a by-product of the way we process information, either structurally, phonemically or semantically.

Libido: any "natural" drive. In sex and gender topics, this refers more specifically to the sex drive and is motivated by the pleasure principle.

Linear perspective: parallel lines such as train tracks appear to get closer together as they recede into the distance.

Longitudinal studies: the same participants are studied over a number of years, even a lifetime, in order to study changes over time.

Long-term memory (LTM): a relatively permanent store that has unlimited capacity and duration. Different kinds of LTM include episodic (memory for personal events), semantic (memory for facts) and procedural (memory for actions and skills).

Masculinity: the behaviours and ideas that are considered to be a characteristic of being male. It is an example of sex typing.

Matched pairs design: research involving two participant groups that consist of pairs of individuals who are as similar as possible (often this is twins). Each pair is divided, and one of each is assigned to each group.

Maternal deprivation: the breaking of the monotropic bond during early childhood.

Method of loci: a memory technique of associating items to be learned with physical locations (e.g. remembering a shopping list

by linking items to where they are in the supermarket).

Mind maps: free-ranging diagrams that use organisation and imagery to encode information so that it can be retrieved more easily.

Monotropy: an innate tendency to form an attachment to one specific individual. This type of attachment is different from all others and much stronger.

Morality: beliefs and values that are shared by a society or a section of society and are the means by which we judge what is right or wrong.

Nativist theory: this theory of perception predicts that we are born with many perceptual capabilities. We simply use them when we need them, even if we have to wait until adulthood. Therefore, perception is encoded in our genetic make-up.

Natural experiment: an experiment where researchers can take advantage of a natural situation in order to carry out an investigation in circumstances that they cannot themselves manipulate.

Naturalistic observation: observing behaviour in a natural, everyday situation, with observers remaining inconspicuous to prevent influence on the behaviour they are observing.

Nature–nurture debate: are we born with our perceptual abilities (nature) or do we learn our perceptual abilities throughout our lives (nurture)?

Negative correlation: a relationship in which as one variable decreases, the other one increases.

Neutral stimulus: any stimulus that causes no response from the organism being conditioned.

Non-participant observation: any observation in which the observer remains separate from the people being observed.

Non-verbal communication (NVC): messages expressed by communication other than linguistic means.

Obedience: behaving in a certain way in response to the demands of an authority figure.

Object permanence: the ability to understand that an object continues to exist even when it is out of sight.

Observation: watching participants' reactions, responses or behaviours within psychological research.

Oedipus complex: the Freudian concept that, during the phallic stage, boys perceive their fathers as a rival for possession of their mother's love.

Oestrogen: the female sex hormone required for sexual development, puberty, the stimulation of egg production and female reproductive organs.

Opportunity sample: consists of participants selected because they are available, not because they are representative of a population.

Order effects: in repeated measures design, the order in which participants do the tasks can affect the results, because of practice, tiredness or boredom.

Organisation: a memory technique that encodes information in a specific way (e.g. always using a yellow sticker on cognitive psychology notes).

Overt observations: observations in which the observers make themselves known to the people being observed (as would be the case for most participant observations).

Participant observation: an observational research method involving active participation within the study group or organisation by the researcher/observer.

Participant variables: possible confounding variables if participants are not as similar as possible, e.g. in age, sex or IQ.

Participants: people who actually participate in psychological research and are vital for research to be carried out. Used to be referred to as "subjects", but this term is no longer in use.

Penis envy: a Freudian concept that occurs when a girl realises she does not have a penis. Argued to be a defining moment in the development of gender and sexual identity for women.

Perception: making sense of and using the information we have stored via our senses. It is about how we interpret this information to make sense of the world.

Perceptual set: a readiness, or a predisposition, to perceive things in a specific way.

Person-centred therapy: a type of therapy whereby a therapist uses the principles of unconditional positive regard, empathy and congruence as a means of helping a client reach self-actualisation.

Phobia: an irrational (unreasonable and illogical) fear of something, someone or some object.

Phonemic/phonetic processing: processing things in relation to how they sound.

Positive correlation: a relationship in which as one variable increases, so does the other one.

Postural echo: a type of non-verbal communication in which people are seen to "mirror" the postures of a partner they are communicating with.

Practice effects: problems associated with participants repeating tasks within research, which may make the task easier for them over time and therefore affect the results.

Pre-operational stage: the second developmental stage, characterised by children learning to visualise objects and events mentally (in their heads).

Preparedness: the idea that organisms have evolved to be frightened of fear-relevant stimuli – those objects or situations that may have been historically life threatening (e.g. rats, spiders, snakes, etc.).

Privation: a situation in which a child has never had the opportunity to form an attachment relationship.

Protection of participants: an ethical guideline stating that researchers must protect participants against psychological and physical harm.

Quasi-experiment: any experiment in which the researcher is unable to manipulate or control variables, therefore not considered to be a "true" experiment.

Questionnaire: a set of questions dealing with any topic. Questions can limit responses (e.g. Are you male or female?) or be open-ended (e.g. Describe your childhood).

Random sample: consists of participants selected on some random basis (e.g. numbers out of a hat). Every member of the population has an equal chance of being selected.

Readjustment studies: research that examines how having to adapt to a new environment affects us psychologically.

Rehearsal: repetition of information in short-term memory to allow encoding into long-term memory (e.g. repeating a phone number in your head).

Relative size: an object's smaller size on your retina means that it is further away from you, and larger objects are seen as being closer.

Repeated measures design: a research design where the same participants are used for all conditions in the experiment.

Representative sample: a sample that is chosen to be typical of the population from which it is drawn.

Retrieval (output): the ability to get information from our memory system in order to use it.

Reversibility: the logical ability to carry out a mental operation that brings something back to its original state. For example, if a child pours water from one container to another of a different shape, it is the ability to be able to mentally pour water back into the original container (reverse the operation) and thereby understand that the amount of water is still the same.

Right to withdraw: an ethical guideline stating that participants can leave the study at any time without penalty, and their data will be destroyed.

Role model: any person whose actions are imitated by the learner; this may be peers, family members or even celebrities.

Sample: the participants actually used in a study, drawn from some larger population.

Scaffolding: the provision of an appropriate support framework for children's learning that can be provided by a more able peer or by an adult.

Secure attachment: a style of attachment that is formed when caregivers respond sensitively to the infant's needs.

Secure base: a concept formulated by John Bowlby to describe the role of the primary caregiver as being a "safe" point to which the child can return when feeling anxiety, fear or distress.

Self-actualisation: the reaching and fulfilling of our own potential.

Self-concept: the mental image that we have of ourselves.

Self-esteem: how we *feel* about our current self.

Semantic processing: processing things in relation to what they mean.

Sensation: our interpretation of the environment around us using touch, taste, smell, sight and sound (the senses).

Sensorimotor stage: the first developmental stage, characterised by children learning to coordinate their sensory experiences (sights, sounds) with their motor behaviours.

Sensory buffer: the first mechanism in Atkinson and Shiffrin's (1972) multistore model of memory. It picks up information that is attended to and sends it to short-term memory.

Separation protest: the distress that young children experience when they are separated from their primary caregiver.

Sex identity: the biological status of being a male or a female.

Sex typing: treating people in accordance with society's expectations of them because of their sex.

Shape constancy: our ability to understand that objects remain the same basic shape, even when viewed from a variety of angles.

Short-term memory (STM): a temporary place for storing information, during which time it receives limited processing (e.g. verbal rehearsal). STM has very limited capacity and short duration, unless the information in it is maintained through rehearsal.

Situational variables: any aspects of the situation that might affect the findings, such as the room, the time of day, the lighting, etc. These must be kept the same for all participants.

Social learning: the process by which an organism "learns" through observation and imitation of the actions of others.

Social learning theory: a theory stating that people learn by observation and imitation of models.

Standardised instructions: the experimenter must give the same instructions to every participant in any one condition.

Standardised procedures: the same procedures are used on every trial of an experiment to ensure that no confounding variables affect the dependent variable.

Storage: the memory system's ability to keep information that we can then use again if necessary.

Stranger anxiety: the distress that young children experience when they are exposed to people who are unfamiliar to them.

Structural processing: processing things in relation to the way they look (e.g. the structure of things).

Structured interview: a list of questions requiring the interviewee to choose from a selection of possible answers.

Superimposition: if one object hides part of another object, then the object that is "complete" is perceived to be closer.

Survey: a research method that allows participants to self-report, via questionnaire or interview, their attitudes/feelings.

Symbolic thought: the ability to have an internal representation (a mental image) of a concept.

Systematic desensitisation: a method of treating phobias, whereby relaxation skills are associated with increasingly phobia-associated stimuli. It works on the principle that relaxation and fear cannot be experienced at the same time.

Systematic sample: consists of participants chosen by a modified version of random sampling in which the participants are selected in a quasi-random way (e.g. every 100th name from a population list).

Target population: the whole group to which a researcher wishes to generalise the findings.

Testosterone: the male sex hormone required for sperm production and the development of male reproductive organs.

Texture gradient: fineness in detail decreases the further away the object is from the eye. So sections of an object or setting become less clear the further away they are.

Token economy: a method of behaviour shaping that rewards appropriate (desired) behaviours with secondary reinforcers (tokens) that can be collected and exchanged for primary reinforcers (something that is wanted).

Top-down processing: stimulus processing that is influenced by factors such as the individual's past experience and expectations.

Trait theory: theory stating that we can categorise people into different personality types.

Unconditional positive regard: when a person is completely accepting of another, no matter what.

Unconditioned stimulus: a stimulus that elicits an involuntary bodily response all on its own, such as dogs dribbling at the sight of food.

Uncorrelated: there is no relationship between two variables, e.g. exam grades and height.

Unstructured interview: an interview beginning with a single question, from which further questions depend on the interviewee's answer.

Verbal communication: involves speech, and can also involve writing since this stands for language.

Vicarious punishment: learning by watching other people being punished rather than being punished directly.

Vicarious reinforcement: learning by watching other people being rewarded rather than being rewarded directly.

Visual illusion: pictures and figures that can be used to trick the perceptual system into seeing something that is not there or perceiving something that is not happening.

Volunteer sample: consists of participants who volunteer to take part in a research study, for instance by replying to an advertisement.

Zone of proximal development: the skill range between what a child can do without help and what they could not achieve even with help.

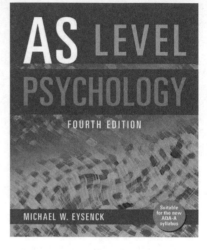